Tectonism

Tectonism

Architecture for the Twenty-First Century

Patrik Schumacher

images Publishing

THE ARTS BRIDGE

Contents

Preface

The idea for this book was conceived in the context of my being awarded the 2021 Designer of the Year by the Arts Bridge, a project of Guangxi Normal University Press, which is committed to the international communication of art, new media, technology, and design. As such it was from the start aimed not only at a generic global architectural audience but more specifically at a Chinese architectural audience. Accordingly, the book is available both in English and Mandarin. China is not only the most important engine of global economic development in general but even of more relative importance with respect to urban and architectural development and trend setting. China is in the midst of a momentous transformation from a manufacturing-based economy—the workshop of the world—to an advanced knowledge economy, the research lab of the world. This implies that China's urban development requirements and solutions are fully relevant to the developed world. It is here that the frontier of innovation can be pushed forward. It is in China where the question about the hegemonic architectural style for the twenty-first century will be decided.

It is the thesis of this book that parametricism in general—and tectonism in particular—is the most viable candidate to become the unified epochal style for the twenty-first century. Implied in this thesis is the subsidiary thesis that the current unresolved pluralism of incompatible styles is something to be overcome rather than to be celebrated. The unity and coherence of our cities are at stake. The fragmentation of the discipline of architecture was originally precipitated by the historical socio-economic shift from Fordism to post-Fordism that undermined the unperturbed continuation of modernist architecture and urbanism. Modernism was no longer viable and the break-up of this paradigm into different search trajectories was initially a natural and necessary development. Forty years later this initial rationale no longer makes sense. This fragmentation has been persisting for so long, despite the fact that a new viable paradigm—congenial to the new societal dynamics—has evolved and matured in the last twenty-five years. This failure of the discipline to converge onto this new viable paradigm—the paradigm of parametricism—is due to the immaturity of the discipline's discourse. The internal theoretical resources and debates are ill prepared to reflect the complexities of the adaptation to recent technological and societal transformations that is required of architecture. I have tried to address this deficit with a prior book-length comprehensive theory of architecture, embedded in a comprehensive theory of society. The current book presupposes the arguments unfolded in the prior book. However, the general gist and key thesis of the prior book—namely the requirement that contemporary architecture must be upgraded via computational empowerment to meet the challenges of the new level of societal complexity and dynamism—is made sufficiently clear in the current book, so that the current treatise is sufficiently freestanding and self-sustaining to make a compelling case on its own, hopefully. What should make tectonism compelling is also all the new sophisticated work that is being presented here.

Patrik Schumacher, London 2022

Introduction

Tectonism is the most advanced and most sophisticated contemporary architectural style. There are, to date, only relatively few fully satisfactory built examples, and most of them are still of a relatively modest scale. Notwithstanding this fact, it is the thesis of this book that tectonism, as defined and illustrated here, represents the future of twenty-first century architecture. This thesis is optimistic with respect to the long-term rationality of the discipline of architecture, i.e., with respect to its capacity to discern and ascertain, via its internal discourse, the superiority of tectonism, and to spread its influence and impact as global best practice accordingly. This optimism also extends to the rationality of the wider society, as represented through private clients, public clients, and through end user acceptance, to be susceptible to the guidance it will receive from architectural expert discourse. This optimism is based on a critical analysis and appraisal of architectural history. The avant-garde methods of the early modernists in the 1920s, backed up by sound theoretical arguments, did win over the discipline in the 1930s and 1940s, and spread its real impact on the global built environment throughout the 1950s, 1960s, and 1970s. The current avant-garde methods within the movement of tectonism, although very different from modernism, are equally well thought through as the arguments in this book will attempt to demonstrate.

As a historical contribution to the development of modern industrial civilization, the modern movement in architecture, now referred to as modernism, was an important and largely successful one. However, it must also be emphasized that this contribution was historically specific, i.e., the real and effective positive contribution of modernist architecture and urbanism made in the twentieth century does not imply the current validity of modernism. Modernism is now largely obsolete, because times have changed due to pervasive computation, with respect to both the architectural requirements of society and architecture's means to address those requirements. The new era requires a new architecture and makes a new architecture possible. The key historical, technology-induced socio-economic shift is the transformation from Fordism, an economy based on rigid mechanical mass production, to post-Fordism based on flexible specialization via reprogrammable machinery and continuously upgraded software as service provisions. This transformation has set workers free from the assembly line and at the same time implies a nearly infinite capacity of the economy to absorb innovations. This in turn implies that all work now potentially becomes self-directed creative work in self-organizing collaborative networks. The implications for urban life and work, and for the building designs that could congenially facilitate the new life, might be summarized as follows: the new complexity, malleability, and dynamism of contemporary life is calling for a matching level of complexity, malleability, and dynamism in its built environment.

This transformation from a Fordist mass society to a post-Fordist network society finds its congenial reflection in the paradigm shift from modernism, via postmodernism and deconstructivism, to parametricism, currently the most promising style in architecture. Parametricism is a well-established, widely circulating label for a broad movement in architecture that has gathered pace and influence since the mid-1990s. I coined the term in 2008. The phenomenon of parametricism, its emergence, theoretical underpinnings, development, and advantages will be explained below in a dedicated chapter. The recent movement and style of tectonism is classified here as a subsidiary style within the overarching epochal style of parametricism. Tectonism is a logical continuation and refinement of earlier stages of parametricism, such as foldism, blobism, and swarmism. Tectonism not only comprises the currently most advanced and sophisticated work within the overarching movement of parametricism but is bound together by a series of new specific principles, fully coherent with the more general principles of parametricism, yet distinct enough to define a new subsidiary style within parametricism. Tectonism is also intuitively recognizable via its distinctive aesthetic characteristics, relative to older versions of parametricism.

Parametricism can be defined as a style where all elements of an architectural composition are parametrically malleable in the pursuit of internal variation and correlation as well as external adaptation. This is achieved via scripts and parametric models that integrate malleable parts into networks of interdependencies. Tectonism is the latest stage of parametricism. Its essential innovation is the utilization of generative algorithms that integrate various form-finding techniques based on engineering logics, including structural optimization, environmental engineering logics as well as new robotic fabrication logics. This integration of engineering knowledge and optimization tools into the initial conception and form generation of a design project implies a major leap forward in design rationality.

This is also a leap forward in complexity and sophistication and thus represents a hurdle for designers who must gain mastery over such an ambitious and difficult methodology. The hurdle is as much conceptual as it is technical. The same also applies, to a lesser extent, to the other subsidiary styles within parametricism. Both parametricism in general and tectonism in particular are sophisticated styles that require initiation, training, hard work, and a steep learning curve. However, optimism is justified by the experience of recent years, namely that an ecosystem of software developers with a keen eye for ease of learning and intuitive use has sprung up to support the movement as well as the abundant proliferation of YouTube tutorials. However, the challenge remains that schools of architecture have to shift away from their current culture of art schools pursuing individualism and novelty toward a more exacting culture of collaborative innovation and professional excellence valuing measurable performance. This includes social performance. In this respect I am working on a methodology of social functionality measurement and optimization via agent-based occupancy simulations.

The development of this new ambitious style and its related methodologies is the product of many years of collective cumulative design research and experimentation, accompanied by a lively expert discourse. The initial intuitions and experiments required the imaginative creativity cultivated by artists, and the current elaboration and realization of the mature style calls more for the creativity and rigor to be cultivated by scientists. This is not to say that design is science. Design, including architectural design, is a sui generis creative culture.

As I argued and elaborated in my book *The Autopoiesis of Architecture*, architecture, together with the other design disciplines that altogether creatively determine the totality of the human phenomenal world, i.e., the total built environment and world of artifacts, constitutes a sui generis function system within society. The societal function of architecture and design is the innovative visual-spatial ordering of societal interactions and communications. As world society, its social order, and modes of interaction progress, so must the visual-spatial framing of these interactions progress in order to remain congenial. This implies the task of continuous upgrading for the design disciplines. If societal progress takes the form of a revolutionary epochal transformation, then a revolutionary shift in epochal style is the appropriate way for the discipline to participate. This was the moment of parametricism. If the societal progress is a matter of moving further along a recently established epochal trajectory, then a cumulative upgrading, deepening, and refinement within an established epochal style is the pertinent way for the design disciplines to contribute to societal progress. This is the path of tectonism in the first half of twenty-first century.

Yet another revolutionary upheaval in architecture and design would only make sense if society is changing direction and transforming systemically. I do not see any such shift on the horizon. The characteristic tendencies of a post-Fordist network society are intensifying and spreading. In any event, there is no sign of a revolutionary new approach or style in architecture and design either. All styles competing with parametricism/tectonism are retro styles, rehashing older approaches, similar to the recycling we often find in fashion: Historicism is a self-proclaimed retrogression, minimalism is a form of neo-modernism, and there is also a recent revival of postmodernism. When it comes to truly original innovation, this is only found within parametricism, and especially in tectonism.

Under contemporary conditions of societal complexity, differentiation, and dynamism, only parametricism—and in particular tectonism—can fulfill the necessary tasks and societal functions of architecture and the design disciplines, namely, to frame and thereby order, articulate, and facilitate the rich variety of simultaneous coordinated social communication scenarios. Design frames social interaction. This was always so, and without an articulate built environment and world of artifacts (including dress systems), no ordered societal process can function. This is a human universal that all human cultures must deliver. The built environment is a societal information process and ordering text. The contemporary versions of this text must be formulated in the language of tectonism. All older languages lack the requisite variety and expressive power and thereby keep urban humanity's progress below its potential, relative to an unleashed super-eloquent, empowering parametric-tectonic urban and architectural environment. This designed environment that orders and frames all communicative interactions also includes all graphic, web-based, and VR-based media environments. The UI and UX designers of our virtual communication platforms are colleagues of us architects who are responding to the same challenges and who should all belong to the same unified discourse of the design disciplines. Parametricsim and tectonism are key reference points for all designers. To grasp what is at stake with respect to the design disciplines' problem domain and task, we need to first set the scene for the discussion of tectonism as the solution.

Architecture's Task: The Designed Environment as Societal Ordering System

The spatial order of the human habitat is both an immediate physical organizing apparatus that separates and connects social actors and their activities, and a material substrate for the inscription of an external "societal memory." These "inscriptions" might at first be an unintended side effect of the various activities routinely unfolding within the habitat. Spatial arrangements are functionally adapted and elaborated. They are then differentially marked and underlined by ornaments, which make them identifiable in a more conspicuous and unmistakable way. The result is the gradual build-up of a spatio-morphological system of signification. Thus, a semantically charged built environment emerges that provides a differentiated system of settings to help social actors orient themselves with respect to the multitude of different communicative situations constituting the social life-process of society. The system of social settings, as a system of distinctions and relations, uses both the positional identification of places (relative location) and the morphological identification of places (ornamental marking) as props for the societal information and communication process. Compelling demonstrations for this formative nexus between social and spatial structure can be found within social anthropology, attesting to the crucial importance of cross-generationally stable spatio-morphological settings for the initial emergence, temporary stabilization, and further evolution of all societies. Only on this basis, with this new material substrate upon which the evolutionary mechanisms of mutation, selection, and reproduction could operate, was the cultural evolution of humankind out of the animal kingdom, and all further cultural evolution, possible.

The built environment orders social processes through its pattern of spatial separations and connections. However, it is important to reflect that the functioning of the desired social interaction scenarios depends on the participants' successful orientation and navigation within the designed environment. The built environment, with its complex matrix of territorial distinctions, is (or should become) a giant, navigable, information-rich interface of communication.

The artificiality and communicative capacity of human settlements, artifacts, and dresses become tangible when we compare the diversity of human visual-material cultures with the visual uniformity of other primate species. The diversity of "artistic" cultures is analogous to the diversity of human languages. Not only are they very different from each other, and largely opaque to each other, but each also comes with its own rich internal differentiations. Visual-artistic cultures are also languages, namely spatio-visual languages. The study of both verbal and visual languages falls under an encompassing discipline, namely "semiotics" or "semiology."

What sets human groups apart from other primates is what we might at earlier times, in the broadest sense, have called art, and what we should now refer to as design. This includes profane and sacred buildings and places, tools and other artifacts, as well all the artistry of decorative self-transformation via dress, jewelry, and make-up. These practices of "artistic" self-transformation are a universal phenomenon of all human groups.

These practices of decoration also include all buildings and artifacts, i.e., in contemporary terms, they include all design disciplines. The significance of these practices, then and now, is the visual marking and thereby conspicuous differentiation of social arenas, roles, and identities without which no social order can be built up or maintained. These props and marks allow dominance hierarchies, as well as more complex societal differentiations, to be institutionalized. The social order becomes independent of the continuous combative physical reestablishment of hierarchy, role differentiation, property, etc. On the basis of this stabilization via built environments and systems of artifacts, the social order also becomes scalable well beyond the size of a primate troop. Design is involved in the elaboration and reproduction of these vital semiological systems.

1. First Premise: Parametricism

In 2008 I first communicated that a new, profound style has been maturing within the avant-garde segment of architecture during the previous ten years. It seemed urgent that the style acquires a name to recognize itself as well as to be recognized in the world at large. Therefore "parametricism" was enunciated during the 11th Venice Architecture Biennale. The term has since been circulating and gathering momentum, initially largely via critical challenges within the architectural discourse. Now it's a well-established, widespread term.

The thesis of this book is that parametricism, and by extension tectonism, is architecture's answer to the challenges and opportunities of the (post-Fordist) information age, just as modernism was architecture's answer to the (Fordist) mechanical age. The challenges that a post-Fordist information society poses to architecture issue from the new diversity and intensive interconnectedness of all social processes. Architecture has to find ways to spatially network diverse, interlocking social processes in legible, high-density agglomerations. The opportunities that the information age offers are the new computationally supported information processing, design, engineering, and fabrication methodologies that can be brought to bear on architecture's new challenges. Parametricism is the only truly original contemporary style, the only style that applies the new opportunities to the new challenges in order to make its genuine contribution to the advancement of world civilization. Parametricism is therefore the only plausible contemporary candidate to become the global epochal style for the twenty-first century. To actively use and assert the concept of style is important.

1.1 The Indispensible Concept of Style

The concept of style in architecture and design is an indispensable orienting category without which discursive self-reflection and self-steering within architecture are stunted.

Outside architectural circles “style” is virtually the only category through which architecture is observed and recognized. A named style needs to be put forward in order to stake the claim to act in the name of architecture.

What complicates matters is that the concept of style(s) has long since been losing traction within the architectural discourse. Therefore, the announcement of parametricism involves two simultaneous discursive moves: the presentation of a new vital architectural movement and the reassertion of the concept of style(s) as a valid and productive category of discursive orientation and self-description.

The concept of style(s) deserves to be defended. To let this concept wither away would only impoverish the discourse within architecture. This would also imply the renunciation of a powerful asset for communicating architecture into society. However, the resuscitation of this drained and battered concept requires conceptual reconstruction in terms that are intellectually credible today.

What stands in the way of such a reconstruction is the tendency to regard style to be merely a matter of appearance as well as the related tendency to confuse styles with superficial, short-lived fashions. Although aesthetic appearance matters enormously in architecture and design, neither architecture as a whole nor its styles can be reduced to mere matters of appearance. Neither must the phenomenon of styles be assimilated to the phenomenon of fashion. The concept of style(s) must therefore be sharply distinguished and cleansed of all these trivializing and distracting connotations. It denotes the unity of the difference between the architectural epochs of the Gothic, Renaissance, baroque, classicism, historicism, and modernism. The historical self-consciousness of architecture demands the revitalization of the concept of style(s) as a profound historical phenomenon that can be projected into the future. For this purpose, I propose that architectural styles are best understood as design research programs conceived in analogy to the way paradigms frame scientific research programs. A new style in architecture/design is akin to a new paradigm in science: It redefines the fundamental categories, purposes, and methods of a coherent collective endeavor. Innovation in architecture proceeds via the progression of styles so understood. This implies the alternation between periods of cumulative advancement within a style and revolutionary periods of transition between styles. Styles represent long, sustained cycles of innovation, gathering the design research efforts into a collective movement so that individual efforts are mutually relevant, spurring, and enhancing.

The question is ultimately one of terminological choice. We could use the concept of paradigm instead. But paradigm is borrowed from the sciences. The concept of style was developed in the late eighteenth- to nineteenth-centuries as a culturally comparative and historical category connected with profound notions like "the spirit of the age" (zeitgeist) and stages of civilization. The concept has also been instrumental in initiating the 100-year-long conscious search for a modern architecture that would be congenial to the modern era. Thus the concept did important historical/progressive work and can still do so now and into the future. It's not reducible to superficial features. The typical characteristics that make styles visually recognizable are just symptoms of a deeper performative reality; after all, we work via form to deliver function, for function's sake, not for the form's sake, but it is on form we must work to deliver performance.

A style's formation and especially its proliferation is initially driven via performative selection criteria. Once established, conscious visual imitation becomes a stabilizing force and an accelerating shortcut for further proliferation. There will be some information loss but a lot of performative features might be preserved in a superficial imitation. However, such a mode of proliferation, although to some extent inevitable, is risky and should be criticized and combatted by the competent protagonists if the information loss is so great that it undermines the superiority and credibility of the style.

From the inside, within architecture, the identification of parametricism/tectonism demarcates and further galvanizes a maturing avant-garde movement and thus might serve to accelerate its progress and potential hegemony as a collective research and development effort. At least this is my hope and motivation. As a piece of retrospective description and interpretation, the announcement of parametricism seems justified given ten years of consistent, cumulative design research. Prospectively the announcement of the style should further consolidate the attained achievements and prepare the transition from avant-garde to mainstream hegemony. I believe that parametricism finally offers a credible, sustainable answer to the drawn-out crisis of modernism that resulted in twenty-five years of stylistic searching. Parametricism is the great new style after modernism. Postmodernism and deconstructivism were mere transitional episodes, similar to art nouveau and expressionism as transitions from historicism to modernism. The distinction of epochal styles from transitional styles is important. In a period of transition there might emerge a rapid succession of styles, or even a plurality of simultaneous, competing styles. The crisis and demise of modernism lead to a deep and protracted transitional period, but this is no reason to believe that this pluralism cannot be overcome by the hegemony of a new unified style. The potential for such a unification is indeed what we are witnessing.

Besides epochal styles and transitional styles we can identify subsidiary styles that emerge under the umbrella of epochal styles. These subsidiary styles represent either parallel variations or historical sequences that enrich and progress the respective epochal style. Within historicism we can distinguish neoclassicism, neo-Gothic, neo-Renaissance, neo-baroque, and ecclecticism. Within modernism we can distinguish functionalism, rationalism, organicism, brutalism, metabolism, and high-tech. All these subsidiary styles adhere fully to the basic design principles of modernism: separation and repetition, i.e., separation between specialized subsystems and repetition within each subsystem. Postmodernism and deconstructivism reject the order of separation and repetition by posing historical diversity and then diversity via collage and superposition (without establishing a new order). Parametricism can recuperate and enhance the deconstructivist moves within a new capacity to create diversity within a complex order. The modernist order of separation and repetition is being supplanted by the parametricist order of continuous differentiation within systems and intensive correlation across systems. Within the broad new paradigm of parametricism, many subsidiary styles might be expected to enrich and progress the coming epoch of parametricism.

We distinguish progress *within* epochal styles from progress *between* epochal styles. Progress between styles is never smooth and implies that one style is being superseded by another, superior, more successful style. What does this superiority or success consist in? Shifts from one dominant style to another might be compared to paradigm shifts in science. Paradigm shifts are usually triggered by a state of crisis within the old paradigm. Such crises are usually brought about by new empirical evidence that overburdens the explanatory capacity of the old paradigm. In the case of styles, it is the emergence of new societal tasks that overburdens the design resources of the old style. Thus, in the case of architectural styles the sense of crisis indicates a state of maladaptation with respect to the societal environment. This occurs when society changes rapidly in ways that invalidate the recipes of the current style. A new style succeeds by affording new problem formulations and solutions that allow architecture to catch up with the new societal developments. Success therefore implies re-adaptation. Sometimes avant-garde architecture is preparing pre-adaptive advances that might even act as catalysts for advances elsewhere in society. The progression of styles is, in this sense, a series of re-adaptations and/or pre-adaptations.

The experience of modernism's crisis and its architectural aftermath—together with the failure to distinguish epochal styles, from transitional and subsidiary styles—has led many critics to believe that our civilization (and today this means global civilization) can no longer be expected to forge a unified style. Did the profound developmental role of styles in the history of architecture as it is evidenced in the sequence Gothic-Renaissance-classicism-baroque-historicism-modernism come to an end? Did history come to an end? Or did it fragment into crisscrossing and contradictory trajectories? If so, are we to celebrate this fragmentation of efforts under the slogan of pluralism?

1.2 Parametricism Against Pluralism

Parametricism is by now manifestly superior to all other styles that are still being pandered to and pursued. This implies that parametricism should sweep the market and put an end to a pluralism of styles (that resulted from modernism's crisis) that has been going on for far too long due to ideological inertia. Perhaps the most obvious argument for the superiority of parametricism is the fact that it is the only style that can take full advantage of the computational revolution that drives contemporary civilization. More specifically it is the only style congenial to recent advances in structural and environmental engineering capacities based on computational analytics and optimization techniques. All other styles are incapable of working with the efficiencies of the adaptive structural and tectonic differentiations that issue from the new engineering intelligence, i.e., they force its adherents to waste this opportunity and thus to waste resources.

More importantly, aside from being the only contemporary style that can efficiently utilize the new technologies of the information age, parametricism is the only contemporary style that can adequately address the new societal tasks posed to architecture by the new social dynamics engendered by the information age.

The plurality of styles must make way for a sweeping parametricism to allow architecture to finally make once more a vital, decisive, transformative impact on the built environment, the way modernism had done in the twentieth century. My arguments about parametricism's superiority and best practice potentials as well as my attendant hope and call for a further convergence of research and design efforts toward the establishment of a unified, hegemonic style that could become the mainstream epochal style of the twenty-first century have been decried as megalomania and an authoritarian imposition threatening to stifle creativity. In contrast to this prejudice, parametricism is inherently open ended and has opened up a whole new huge and inexhaustible universe of possibilities for fresh creative explorations, while closing down only the worn-out and comparatively miniscule realms of classicism and modernism as well as the already self-retired realms of postmodernism and deconstructivism. I certainly neither can, nor wish to impose anything. I communicate in the hope of finding potential collaborators in a venture that can only take off as a collective process where best-practice principles emerge from the bottom up and then (hopefully) constrain and direct a cumulative research and innovation process.

The pluralist a priori that all styles are equally valid is nothing but a comforting and false dogma. The fallacy of celebrating a pluralism of styles is an analogue of the fallacy of multiculturalism and a misconceived child of the same intellectual milieu, an intellectual milieu blunted by a PC politeness that prefers to gloss over realities with euphemisms rather than to confront them. The difficulty of analyzing an increasingly complex world and the difficulty of consistently arguing about the merits and demerits of (irreconcilable) styles leads to the pretence that all styles are equally "valid," a pathetic abdication of intellectual ambition and responsibility, pervasive among today's "thinking people." Pluralism makes sense only temporarily in periods of searching transition: when contestants are in competition to find and establish the new superior style and best practice that deserves to become pervasive. This was the period of postmodernism and deconstructivism after the bankruptcy of modernism. Set permanently as an end and value in and of itself, pluralism spells stagnation. Pluralists (like multiculturalists) are too tolerant for too long in the sense of giving blanket intellectual cover to all manner of dysfunctional retro styles and intellectually bankrupt values. Tolerance toward backwardness helps nobody, not even those who have been laggard; and this includes all those architectural tribes, architects, and would-be architects who lock themselves out of the advances of our new computationally augmented civilization due to prejudice, lack of insight, and effort, and not least due to the pervasive, lazy, and paralyzing ideology of (multi-culturalist) pluralism that has outlived its temporary usefulness already for two decades and has thus become a fetter on our further progress.

Styles are not neutral with respect to societal progress, i.e., with respect to advancing productivity, prosperity, and freedom. While the real productivity of the competing styles will be tested in terms of the comparative market success of architects (and ultimately of their clients), the prospective productivity of competing styles can be theoretically analyzed. This possibility must be granted before we can even start debating the direction forward.

The existence of a unified, hegemonic style and thus the existence of a coherent language of architecture would facilitate the overall legibility, and hence global navigability, of the built environment. The multiplicity of competing styles is in no way correlated with the multiplicity of substantial functions that need to be accommodated and articulated. Thus, stylistic multiplicity produces visual noise. A dominant style, with a consistent pattern of establishing form-function relations, facilitates the effective semiosis of a language that can orient and inform users.

A permanent pluralism of styles spells architectural stagnation and urban disarticulation. The discipline's discourse should aim at arriving at a result that can steer us forward in a coherent direction rather than allowing the myriad architectural interventions that make up the city to contravene each other's agendas. The idea of a methodological hegemony or a pervasive global best-practice ethos is nothing scary. It unleashes rather than stifles truly innovative and impactful creativity. Parametricism implies the enhancement of both order and freedom in comparison with all prior styles. The universe of possibilities and new creative opportunities it opens up are exhilarating. The apt analogy here is with the "endless forms of nature." Here, too, richness evolves on the basis of rigorous laws of nature. The multi-author accumulation of an intricately layered and correlated urban order can be viewed in analogy to the evolution of a complex ecosystem. This has very little in common with marching in unison—this was modernism's version of hegemony—but much more with an ecology of different co-evolving species and life-forms. Each architect's new urban intervention can be compared with the evolution of a new species that finds its own way and scripts according to which it registers, adapts, and resonates in the given urban ecology. Think of a certain species of moss growing over a rock formation and accentuating the rock's shallower slopes. What is excluded is a random, wilful, arbitrary imposition that disrupts the city's evolving intricate texture, like garbage thrown into nature. What is demanded instead is that the new contribution resonates and thus communicates with its context by scripting its solution as a function of what it encounters. However, the way a new intervention transcodes and accentuates what is there—by amplification, inversion, camouflage or whatever else—is a matter of the architect-author's creative invention. Let an ecology of a thousand flowers bloom, but let us prevent the current pluralist garbage spill pollution that is choking us everywhere.

Architecture today is world architecture. Every architectural project is immediately exposed and assessed in comparison to all other projects. Global convergences are possible. This does not spell homogenization and monotony. It merely implies a consistency of principles, ambitions, and values to build upon so that different efforts add up, are relevant to each other, compete constructively with each other, to establish the conditions for cumulative progress, rather than pursuing contradictory efforts that misconstrue and deny each other, or going round in circles by continuously battling over fundamentals. This is the idea of a unified style, initially as a unified avant-garde design research program, and eventually as a unified system of principles, ambitions, and values that constitute global best practice.

1.3 Parametricism and Progress

Many critics of parametric design and parametricism ask: What is the societal relevance of the complex geometries and intricate spatial compositions made possible by parametric design? Is this not an expensive, indulgent, and self-serving narcissism on the part of designers that distracts from the social task of architecture? This question must be answered, and in order to answer this question, we need to clarify the societal function of architecture and urban design: the spatial ordering of social processes. The increasing density, diversity, and interconnectedness of contemporary life processes require complex spatial configurations that allow a diversity of event scenarios to unfold in close proximity and awareness of each other. The required complex spatial organizations can only function if the participants that need to come together in the various event scenarios can successfully orient and navigate the spaces they encounter. This requires architectural articulation. The general characteristics of parametricism, such as curvelinearity, gradients, and correlative resonances are potentially more effective in the legible articulation of the desired multitude of relations between the networked spaces. Without curves, smooth transitions, and gradients the complex urban scene quickly degenerates into visual chaos. The urban subsystems that might be correlated via rule-based associative scripts might include the differentiated urban massing, topography, vehicular circulation, and pedestrian circulation. The establishment of systematic dependencies via rule-based design processes increases the information density of the built environment because every dependency chain can be traced back via inferences. The designer might choose and calibrate the adaptive correlations between the internally differentiated subsystems so that the different systems do indeed become "representations" of each other in the sense that users navigating the urban environment can not only follow the gradients (vectors of transformation) in each of the subsystems, but can infer the visible from the not yet visible and invisible systems, for instance when the silhouette of the urban massing might "represent" the underlying topography, it then allows the street- and path-network to be inferred. Similarly, within a mixed-use complex the differentially articulated structural system might represent or indicate the program distribution. The result could be an intricately ordered and thus information-rich environment as a permanent broadcast and powerful social ordering apparatus that facilitates the intricate process of social cooperation. My dream is a built environment that is so rigorously differentiated and correlated like a natural environment where, e.g., the river's path can be inferred from the topography, where the river together with topography and sun orientation differentiate the flora and where the fauna can be inferred from the flora and thus allows animals to navigate and home in on their vital resources via their cognitive information processing. The most primitive example is perhaps the bacteria's path along a nutrition gradient. The most complex and sophisticated version should be the human browsing of information-rich urban environments with the deep relationality we can expect from the skilful and careful application of the principles of parametricism. We should be able to navigate cities and home in on the vital social resources distributed within it with the same assuredness that characterizes animal navigation, with the same kind of subliminal cognitive processing, i.e., in a "state of distraction" rather than via an effortful deciphering of signage or maps. The whole built environment must become a 360-degree interface of multimodal communication, as the ability to navigate dense and complex urban environments has become a crucial aspect of today's overall productivity.

A corollary of this design methodology would be the emergence of intricately beautiful cityscapes and unique urban identities instead of the current ugly and menacing visual chaos and disorienting, identity-less white noise sameness that is the result of the current "garbage spill urbanization." The enhancement of the communicative capacity of the built environment via rule-based parametric design thus goes to the heart of architecture's societal function of ordering the network of social interaction scenarios that make up contemporary society.

However, admittedly the parametric design community is still flexing its muscles rather than going to work with a clear social purpose. In many young design studios and schools of architecture, the playful exploration of new parametric tools results in designs that cannot yet stand up to the critical scrutiny of the sceptics that demand to see the societal relevance and social performance of design efforts. The strategic societal utilization of parametric design becomes an urgent agenda that must be explicitly posed and addressed within the parametric design movement. Self-criticism based on the explicit formulation of the key task is crucial: the ordering of the complexity of social life processes via complex, legible, information-rich spatial orders. The continued credibility of parametricism is at stake. However, we must also protect the need for continued playfulness in the exploration of new tools, techniques, and repertoires. Innovation requires the oscillation between open-ended exploration, determinate testing, and rigorous attempts at successful practical application.

1.4 Conceptual and Operational Definition of Parametricism

As a conceptual definition of parametricism one might offer the following formula: Parametricism implies that all architectural elements and complexes are parametrically malleable. This implies a fundamental ontological shift within the basic, constituent elements of architecture. Instead of the classical and modern reliance on ideal (hermetic, rigid) geometrical figures—straight lines, rectangles, as well as cubes, cylinders, pyramids, and (semi-)spheres—the new primitives of parametricism are animate (dynamic, adaptive, interactive) geometrical entities—splines, nurbs, and subdivs—as fundamental geometrical building blocks for dynamical systems like "hair," "cloth," "blobs," and "metaballs," etc., that react to "attractors" and can be made to resonate with each other via scripts (Figs. 1–4).

Figs. 1–4: Classical/ modernist ontology (Le Corbusier) versus parametricist ontology (Zaha Hadid Architects)

In principle every property of every element or complex is subject to parametric variation. The key technique for handling this variability is the scripting of functions that establish associations between the properties of the various elements. However, although the new style is to a large extent dependent upon these new design techniques, the style cannot be reduced to the mere introduction of new tools and techniques. What characterizes the new style are new ambitions and new values—both in terms of form and in terms of function—that are to be pursued with the aid of the new tools and techniques. Parametricism pursues the very general aim to organize and articulate the increasing diversity and complexity of social institutions and life processes within the most advanced center of a post-Fordist network society. For this task parametricism aims to establish a complex variegated spatial order. It uses scripting to lawfully differentiate and correlate all elements and subsystems of a design. The goal is to *intensify the internal interdependencies* within an architectural design as well as the *external affiliations and continuities* within complex, urban contexts. Parametricism offers a new, complex order via the principles of differentiation and correlation.

This general verbal and motivational definition of parametricism can and must be complemented by an operational definition. It is necessary to operationalize the intuitive values of a style in order to make its hypotheses testable, to make its dissemination systematic, to be exposed to constructive criticism, including self-critique of the parametricist design work, etc.

The operational definition of a style must formulate general instructions that guide the creative process in line with the general ambitions and expected qualities of the style. A style is not only concerned with the elaboration and evaluation of architectural form. Each style poses a specific way of understanding and handling functions. Accordingly, the operational definition of parametricism comprises both formal heuristics—establishing rules and principles that guide the elaboration and evaluation of the design's formal development and resolution—as well as functional heuristics—establishing rules and principles that guide the elaboration and evaluation of the design's functional performance.

For each of these two dimensions the operational definition formulates the heuristics of the design process in terms of operational taboos and dogmas specifying what to avoid and what to pursue. At the same time these heuristic design guidelines provide criteria of self-critique and continuous design enhancement.

Operational definition of parametricism

FORMAL HEURISTICS

Negative principles (taboos):	• avoid rigid forms (lack of malleability) • avoid simple repetition (lack of variety) • avoid collage of isolated, unrelated elements (lack of order)
Positive principles (dogmas):	• all forms must be soft (intelligent: deformation = information) • all systems must be differentiated (gradients) • all systems must be interdependent (correlations)

FUNCTIONAL HEURISTICS

Negative principles (taboos):	• avoid rigid functional stereotypes • avoid segregatiing functional zoning
Positive principles (dogmas):	• all functions are parametric activity/event scenarios • all activities/events communicate with each other

The avoidance of the taboos and the adherence to the dogmas deliver complex, variegated order for complex social institutions. These principles outline pathways for the continuous critique and improvement of the design. The designers can always increase the coherence and intricacy of their design by inventing further variables (degrees of freedom) for the compositions' primitive components. There is always scope for the further differentiation of the arrays or subsystems that are made up by the elemental primitives. This differentiation can be increased with respect to the number of variables at play, with respect to the range of differences it encompasses and with respect to the fineness and differential rhythm of its gradients. There is always further scope for the correlation of the various subsystems at play in the multisystem set-up. Ultimately every subsystem will be in a relationship of mutual dependency with every other subsystem, directly or indirectly; and the number of aspects or properties of each subsystem that are involved in the network of correlation might be increased with each design step. Further there is always the possibility (and often the necessity) to add further subsystems or layers to the (ever more complex and intricate) composition. Also, it is always possible to identify further aspects or features of the (principally unlimited) urban context that might become an occasion for the design to register and respond to. Thus the context sensitivity of the design can be increased with every design step. Thus the heuristics of parametricism will direct a trajectory of design intensification that is in principle an infinite task and trajectory. There is always a further possibility of pushing up the intensity, coherence, intricacy, and beauty of the design. As the network of relations tightens, each further step becomes more elaborate, more involved as all the prior subsystems and their trajectories of differentiation should ideally be taken into account. Arbitrary additions show up conspicuously as alien disruptions of the intricate order elaborated so far. Each additional element or subsystem that enters the composition at a late, highly evolved stage challenges the ingenuity of the designer, and more so the more the design advances. The complex, highly evolved design assumes increasingly the awesome air of necessity or quasi-nature. However, the design remains open ended. There can be no closure. The classical concepts of completeness and perfection do not apply to parametricism. Parametricism's complex variegated order does not rely on the completion of a figure. It remains an inherently open composition.

The consistency of the style as a collective design research program depends upon the unfailing adherence to these strictures and impositions. (The good news is that a whole generation of young architects is already unfailingly adhering to these strictures and impositions [taboos and dogmas] of parametricism—whether this is always explicitly reflected or not.) Any unprincipled vacillation or compromise in this respect—falling back upon old, suspended solutions—compromises the status of the design as rigorous avant-garde design research hypothesis. The principles have to be upheld tenaciously—even in the face of initial difficulties and failures—for the sake of giving radical innovation a chance. Without this tenacity and without the attendant methodological tolerance of failures a culture gets stuck in local maxima.[1]

Rigorous adherence to the principles across all design tasks is a necessary condition to test parametricism's claim of universal competency. However, beside this methodological argument there there is an important substantial reason to insist on absolute consistency. The performative advantage of parametricism over all prior styles is premised on this consistency of adherence to its principles. This is so because parametricism's ability to set up continuities and correspondences across many diverse and distant elements relies on its principles holding uninterrupted sway. Only this way can perceptual orientation and navigability be maximized in the face of everybody's requirement to participate in increasingly diverse and complex life processes. Parametricism allows for the design of information-rich environments. When all elements are part of differentiated subsystems, and these differentiations are lawful (algorithmic) and thus retrievable, as well as correlated with many other differentiations, then the various differentiated subsystems become each other's representations. In such a dense network of associations that radiate deep through the urban fabric many system-to-system (locale-to-locale) inferences as well as local-to-global inferences become possible. The pervasiveness of parametricist interdependencies does not at all imply monotony or homogeneity. It also does not imply that large parts of the city must be designed

1 The discipline has differentiated into avant-garde and mainstream in order to escape from local maxima via high-risk test projects. The avant-garde segment functions as a zone where high-risk strategies are rewarded and partial, temporary dysfunctionality is tolerated.

by a single design team or even that there must be a master plan that integrates individual efforts. It only implies that the continuities that have been forged should not be disrupted by the intervention of non-parametricist designers. Parametricist continuation is always possible in myriad, unpredictable, and qualitatively diverse ways, but it is never random. Satisfying parametricist continuation is admittedly a difficult and elaborate process that demands a high level of talent (or acquired sensibility) and technical expertise. Fortunately, however, the community of designers that is gearing up for the task is growing by the day. Parametricist urbanism is delivering a variegated, complex order where older styles can only either suppress contemporary social complexity or descend into visual chaos.

As alluded to above, many theorists—such as Charles Jencks, and others—have presumed that the demise of modernism ushered in an era of stylistic pluralism. Accordingly, the search for a new, unified style is seen as an anachronism. Any style today—so it seems—can only be one among many other simultaneously operating styles, thus adding one more voice to the prevailing cacophony of many voices. The idea of a pluralism of styles is just one symptom of the more general trivialization and denigration of the concept of style indicated earlier. I repudiate the complacent acceptance (and even celebration) of the apparent pluralism of styles as a supposed sign of our times. A unified style has many advantages over a condition of stylistic fragmentation. Parametricism is therefore posed to aim for hegemony and combats all other styles.

The admixture of a postmodernist, deconstructivist, or minimalist design can only disrupt the penetrating and far-reaching parametricist continuity. The reverse does not hold because there is no equivalent degree of continuity in postmodernist, deconstructivist, or minimalist urbanism. In fact, parametricism can take up vernacular, classical, modernist, postmodernist, deconstructivist, and minimalist urban conditions and forge a new network of affiliations and continuities between and beyond any given number of urban fragments and conditions.

1.5 Style War: Parametricism Versus Minimalism

What are the current styles that must be combated by parametricism? Is there really still the kind of stylistic pluralism posited by Charles Jencks? In fact, postmodernism has disappeared. The same goes for deconstructivism. (The contributions/advances of both have been incorporated within parametricism.) The mainstream, in fact, has returned to a form of pragmatic modernism with a slightly enriched palette: a kind of modernist eclecticism mixing and matching elements from all of modernism's subsidiary styles. The inability of postmodernism and deconsructivism to formulate a new viable paradigm led to the return of modernism, in the guise of two variants: minimalism as the principled, pronounced re-enactment and even radicalization of modernism on the one hand, and the unprincipled, pragmatic, diffuse variant one might call pragmatic modernism. Minimalism operates as intensely ideological, i.e., as intransigent, as parametricism (although it does so without explicit theory). Perhaps the best example is David Chipperfield's impressive oeuvre. Minimalism operates with taboos and dogmas that are as sharply defined as those of parametricism. In contrast, pragmatic modernism is introduced here nearly as a residual category. It contains everything else that goes on today, including all mainstream work. This does not imply that the term "pragmatic modernism" is to be taken in any way derogatory. We also include here the brilliant work of OMA and its spin-offs. However, the primary confrontation in the struggle for stylistic hegemony is the confrontation between parametricism and minimalism. Minimalism is nothing but a sophisticated neo-modernism. The confrontation between parametricism and minimalism is thus the confrontation of a progressive, untested hypothesis with a regressive harking back to a refuted paradigm that had flourished for fifty years but later had experienced a major crisis, and thus proved unsustainable as a universal style for our contemporary era.

Parametricism is claiming universal validity. It cannot be dismissed as eccentric signature work that only fits high-brow cultural icons. No, all moments of contemporary life become uniquely individuated within a continuous, ordered texture.

Mountain Train, Innsbruck, Austria,
Zaha Hadid Architects 2004–2007

Figs. 5–8: Four stations for the Mountain Train Innsbruck, Austria, Zaha Hadid Architects 2004–2007

The latest built works from Zaha Hadid Architects are much more than experimental manifesto projects, they are succeeding as high-performance projects in the real world. The Innsbruck train stations are a good example (Figs. 5–8). No other style could have achieved this coincidence of adaptive variation to the different site conditions with genotypical coherence across those phenotypical variants. Large-scale projects in Beijing, Cairo, and Seoul (Fig. 9) prove that parametricism is able to deliver all the components for a high-performance contemporary life process. Parametricism is ready to go mainstream. The style war has begun.

Fig. 9: Dongdaemon Design Centre plaza and park, Seoul, Korea Zaha Hadid Architects 2007–2014

2. Second Premise: Computational Engineering

Structural engineering science radically transformed its ontology and methodology from a typological to a topological paradigm. This implies a radical reset of the categories that guide engineering practice. The modern forms of engineering rationality based on system types are now exposed as inefficient while the rationality of older structural forms based on slowly evolved traditions is now revealed by the new paradigm. These forms—like the Gothic cathedrals—often offer higher degrees of efficiency that were not verifiable via calculations before the advent of the computational revolution in engineering science. Beyond this revelation and recuperation of pre-modern, more differentiated and integrated solutions, we witness the proliferation of radically new forms that the new paradigm makes possible. This radical expansion of structural possibilities—mirroring the endless forms of nature—is congenial with the requirements of contemporary architectural design where a much higher degree of versatility is required to meet the challenges of a much more complex society.

We are living in an increasingly dynamic and complex world where social institutions, social types and identities proliferate, hybridize, and indeed seem to blend into each other, into a continuously differentiated social texture. Stable stereotypes dissolve and fixed hierarchies everywhere have given way to fluid networks, both in our private and working lives. We might summarize this by saying that our modern social typology has given way to a postmodern condition of social *topology*.[2]

This new fluid societal condition has a material base: the fourth industrial revolution[3] with its ever more pervasive use of digital

2 The originally mathematical concept of topology implies gradual variation and transformation, and its metaphorical expansion can thus serve us here as a suggestive counter concept to the concept of typology.

3 Klaus Schwab, "The Fourth Industrial Revolution," (World Economic Forum, 2016).

computing power crunching through ever bigger data sets in the quest for ever more subtly tailored adaptive product and service optimizations. This new social life process is also demanding a new congenial built environment, equally differentiated and fluid; and naturally this new built environment can be delivered only via upgraded architectural and engineering disciplines that are equally empowered by the new digital computing powers. The new condition implies that each new construction project is characterized by both complexity and novelty. Routine solutions are out of the question. R&D is now always involved. This implies a closer collaboration between the various contributors: developers, architects, and engineers.

2.1. Collaboration and Distinction Between Architecture and Engineering

With respect to the innovative design of built environments the design team is structured along the demarcation line of design versus engineering. The same basic dividing line exists with respect to product design, and indeed all design disciplines, including fashion design. With respect to the built environment the engineering side of the project is internally differentiated into an ever-increasing number of different engineering specialisms. However, the primary dividing line here is the differentiation into architecture versus engineering. This dividing line emerged over the last 200 years and finally resulted in two distinct, autonomous, even incommensurable discourses, or to be more precise, in the terminology of my theory of architectural autopoiesis, *autopoietic systems of communications*.[4] Architecture and engineering—or more generally the design disciplines versus the engineering sciences—constitute distinct domains of competency that can now be sharply defined, each with its own unique responsibilities, concepts, methods, values, and criteria of success. These discursive domains can be subsumed under Niklas Luhmann's category of *societal function systems* (Funktionssysteme).[5] According to Luhmann,

---

4 Patrik Schumacher, *The Autopoiesis of Architecture, Volume 1: A New Framework for Architecture* (London: John Wiley & Sons Ltd., 2010).

5 Niklas Luhmann, *Social Systems*, (California, United States: Stanford University Press, 1995); original: *Soziale Systeme: Grundriss einer allgemeinen Theorie* (Frankfurt, 1984); see also Niklas Luhmann, *Die Desellschaft der Gesellschaft,* Vols. 1 and 2 (Frankfurt am Main, 1998).

modern ("functionally differentiated") society is operating as the co-evolution of autonomous, self-referentially closed systems of communications, such as the economic system, the political system, the legal system, the system of the sciences, the art system, etc. Each of these function systems serves a unique, societal function and claims exclusive and universal responsibility/competency within its respective domain. It is one of the premises of the theory of architectural autopoiesis that architecture (together with the other design disciplines) constitutes a great, societal function system in the precise sense Luhmann had defined with respect to the other societal domains listed above.[6] This implies that the demarcation between architecture and engineering is to be drawn much sharper than the (internal) distinctions that might be drawn among design disciplines or within the engineering disciplines. Architecture might temporarily fuse with interior design and furniture design, which in turn might morph into product and fashion design. Here demarcations are a matter of degree and individual emphasis. The key concepts and values are basically the same. The same overlap condition applies to the distinction of, e.g., structural and façade engineering, or between services engineering and sustainability engineering. Again, the concepts and values are basically the same in all engineering disciplines. In contrast, the demarcation between architecture/design versus engineering/science is sharply drawn and ultra-stable. We should not expect any discursive synthesis here. Instead, we should expect and work toward the clarification and further sharpening of the demarcation, in terms of the distinct competencies and criteria of success of each side. For instance, in recent years the engineering support also routinely involves façade engineering. Engineers now also get involved in the technical detailing of the interior surfaces. These aspects had some years ago still resided in the domain of the architect's expertise. This demonstrates that the distillation of architecture's inalienable core competency continues.

6 Luhmann failed to recognize architecture/design's unique discourse and societal raison d'être. He committed the anachronism of categorizing architecture as one of the arts within the art system. However, art and architecture finally (and decisively) severed their (formerly indeed united) discourses during the first half of the twentieth century.

There is no doubt that progress with continuously increasing performance—in general as well as in relation to the built environment—implies the need for an intensified specialization and collaboration of the specialists in interdisciplinary expert teams. However, interdisciplinary work does not imply the dissolution of disciplinary boundaries. While individual careers might migrate across disciplinary boundaries, effective interdisciplinarity demands that at any time the different competencies that are expected to contribute to the overall success of the project are clearly demarcated. The premise of our contribution here is thus a double thesis that implies both the strictest demarcation and the closest collaboration between architecture and engineering as preconditions for the productive advancement of the built environment. The underlying division of labor might be posited as follows: Architecture is responsible for the built environment's social performance. Engineering is responsible for the built environment's technical performance. Technical performance is a basic precondition of social performance. In this sense engineering might be argued to be primary. Social performance is the goal. In this sense architecture might be argued to be primary. Thus, the relation cannot be brought into a hierarchy. Rather it is a relation of mutual dependency and dialectical advancement. Architectural goals must be defined within a technically delimited space of possibilities. Engineering research and development thus expands the universe of possibilities that constrains architectural invention. However, it cannot be taken for granted that engineering research and development expands the universe of possibilities in relevant, desired directions without being prompted and inspired by architectural goals. In turn, architectural goals and inventions might be prompted and inspired by recent engineering advances. The two disciplines co-evolve in mutual adaptation. Evidence of this can be found in the congeniality between the architectural avant-garde style of parametricism and structural engineering's contemporary capacity to calculate and optimize, smoothly differentiated structures. However, we must reflect on the fact that for us architects these differentiated structures enter our considerations as just another set of compositional elements in our quest to differentiate the spatial scene in accordance with the differentiation of social situations. Congeniality does not imply the conflation of concerns and competencies.

2.2. Structural Fluidity: From Typology to Topology in Structural Engineering

The digital revolution that brought a series of powerful new design tools into architecture has also provided structural engineering with new tools to analyze and calculate structures; in a manner that is congenial to the architectural ambition toward parametric variability that has been unleashed by the new digital design tools. Traditional and twentieth-century modern architecture was a game of assembling simple platonic forms, such as cuboids, cylinders, spheres, and pyramids. The key characteristic of contemporary architecture that challenges engineering is the pursuit of complex and continuously changing forms. Such fluid forms can no longer be analyzed by means of decomposing them into discrete elements and establishing clear-cut structural systems. This is significant because it challenges structural engineering with respect to its most basic elements and concepts.

Figs. 10–11: Mies van der Rohe, Crown Hall, Illinois Institute of Technology, Chicago, United States 1956. The primary structure here uses the portal frame as the distinct structural system type. A sequence of large-span portal frames—bound together by secondary beams—makes up the structure.

Classical modern structural engineering—in distinction to contemporary engineering—relies on the ability to decompose any structure into clear and independent structural subsystems and elemental members. Each subsystem adheres to standard concepts, such as column, beam, cantilever, portal frame, arch, slab, barrel vault, dome, and so on (Figs. 10–11). This typology was taken to be definitive. Each of these concepts is characterized by a clearly typified geometric schema with its attendant configuration of loads, supports, and forces. Each can be further characterized by more detailed system choices, i.e., a beam might be articulated as truss, Vierendeel beam, or box beam, and so on. Within each simple subsystem the active forces can be easily ascertained, and great care is taken to control the transfer of forces from subsystem to subsystem by the precise articulation of the joints that only transmit a particular, well-defined force. The overall arrangement of forces can then be traced step by step. This strategy of clear and distinct decomposition sacrifices efficiency and redundancy for analytical clarity and tractability. This strategy of decomposition is then aligned with the strategy of uniformity within each system, eschewing differentiation. Both decomposition and uniformity are strategies for the reduction of complexity that recognizes the narrow computational capacity of the pre-digital era. Uniformity also recognizes the industrial fabrication system of the Fordist era (Figs. 12–13).

Figs. 12–13: Mies van der Rohe, National Gallery, Berlin, Germany 1968. The structure is a beam grid on eight columns with hinge joints. In both examples the modern structural principles are clearly in evidence: Distinct system type, uniformity, decomposition into discrete elements with controlled load/force transmission at the joints. Yet another aspect of modern engineering becomes evident here: these principles owe their historical rationality as much to the Fordist fabrication logic of mechanical mass reproduction of standardized industrial elements like the I-beam.

In contrast to this modern typological approach, contemporary engineering has become topological and can thus better serve the new architectural style that aims to create spaces that are morphing different spatial sections into a seamlessly differentiated continuum that resists any decomposition into discrete spaces that could be conveniently structured by discrete structural systems. In traditional structures the ability to analyze and calculate the behavior of the structure is premised upon the purity of structural type and the severing of all redundant connections. However, conceptually distinct structural system types—beam versus arch, and so on—are disappearing from engineering due to the new modeling techniques, like Finite Element Analysis. We thus witness a radical conceptual shift—a paradigm shift—within engineering. This is also an ontological shift as it revolutionizes the most basic entities that constitute a structure. I would like to call this paradigm shift the shift from typology to topology. It is at the same time a conceptual shift from parts to particles with respect to the mode of decomposition for calculation. This shift in structural engineering has not been triggered by the new architectural style but rather follows from the internal logic of structural science in the pursuit of structural optimization, in combination with the computational empowerment that makes this pursuit feasible.

A very similar but initially independent shift has also transformed architecture: the pursuit of higher levels of variation and complexity in response to the new societal conditions, again in combination with the computational empowerment that makes this pursuit feasible.[7] It is precisely the idea of typology—the thinking in clearly defined spatial types—that is also disappearing from contemporary architecture, especially within the movement and style of parametricism. In fact, "From Typology to Topology" was one of the early key slogans of the tendency within contemporary architecture that has since (since 2008) been termed parametricism. This implies that contemporary architecture escapes all modern engineering procedures. With new engineering tools like FEA, which break the structures into particles rather than into parts, the engineer is able to capture the ever-shifting arrangement of forces. The universe of potential force patterns becomes boundless.

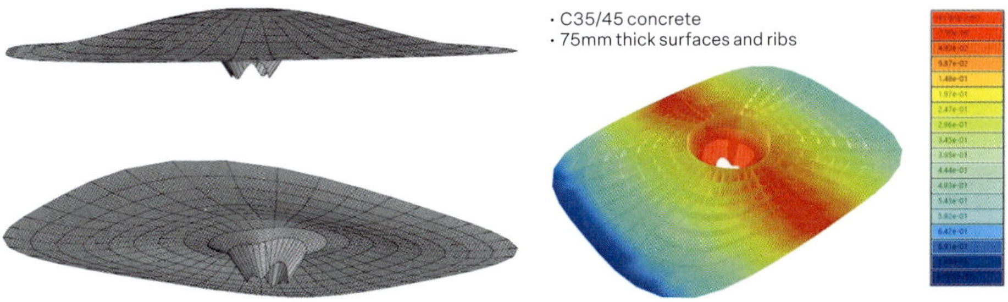

Figs. 14–15: Mushroom-roof detail of a villa project, undisclosed location, Zaha Hadid Architects

This mushroom-like roof structure follows no standard structural system type. The integration of structural analysis via FEA during the design process allows for structural feedback during the sculpting process. The stress distributions and deformational impact is modeled and becomes dependent upon the differentiated sectional profile. This is a first step toward optimization. Here structural calculation is not reduced to identify critical points that determine the dimension of a priori forms but all points become potentially "critical" points.

---

7 It becomes clear here that the invention and proliferation of computational information technology has been the decisive original underlying factor that has been and still is transforming not only architecture and engineering but all disciplines and arenas of professional and social life, and thus underlies the global transformation of society.

The mushroom roof detail of a villa project shown here (Figs. 14–15) is similar to (but more complex) than Félix Candela's concrete umbrella roofs. What Candela achieved via empirical test series, namely an optimized thickness distribution, can now be computed via FEA.

"From Parts to Particles" is another key slogan of contemporary architecture. Structural engineers can now analyze mixed hybrid systems. A tool like FEA can also cope with dense, redundant

Figs. 16–17: Phaeno Science Center, Wolfsburg, Germany, Zaha Hadid Architects 2000–2005. Two structural systems—the waffle slab for the main floor and the Vierendeel space frame for the roof—are correlated via the structural cones as inhabitable megacolumns. Both systems are non-uniform subsystems, whereby the space frame is more subtly and extensively differentiated as the structural grid lines fan in both directions in adaptation to the trapezoidal global roof shape. Each cell of the Vierendeel space frame is thus unique, and each member profile is individually sized according to the varied load conditions.

interrelations of the parts of a structure. We no longer need to sever and isolate the structural components or subsystems. This means that we can harness the structural efficiency of an interconnected network, where parts work together rather than remain independent from each other. The re-tooled engineer allows the structural forces to flow freely through the surfaces provided by the architect. This is the era of structural fluidity.

It thus becomes evident that the architectural style of parametricism is congenial with the most advanced (topologically based) engineering thinking, and indeed that parametricism is the only style that fully utilizes the new engineering intelligence.

I would like to cite Zaha Hadid Architects' Phaeno Science Center in Wolfsburg, Germany, as an early example where the structural systems morph as much as the architectural forms (Figs. 16–17). Here we can observe a mixture of spanning, cantilevering, and vaulting within a waffle slab, whereby spans and cantilevering dimensions are continuously changing. The cones flare into the waffle slab rather than remain discreet props that pick up their load at distinct points of contact. The space frame above is continuously differentiated whereby each member within the space frame has a different angle (the grid fans in two directions) so that each cell of the space frame has a different size. In a complementary move each member has a different thickness and weight. Obviously, this nuanced optimization can only be coped with by means of computers, both with respect to the calculation of forces as well as with respect to the handling of the complex geometry and manufacturing schedules.

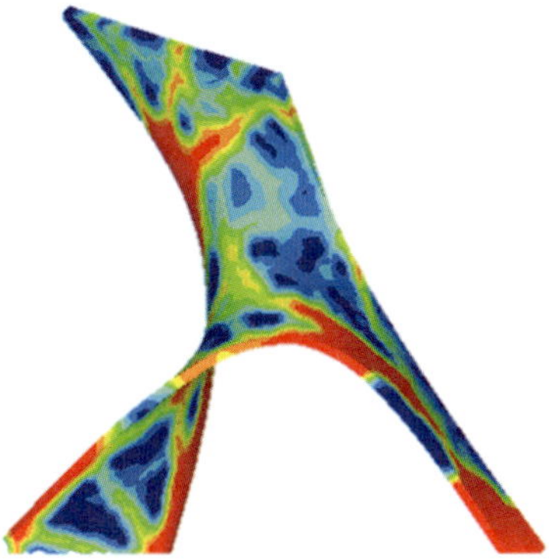

Figs. 18–19: Experimental structure using a shell form as the basis for the operation of the application of the topology optimization algorithm; Zaha Hadid Architects' CODE group. Mexico City, Mexico 2013. Here the perforation pattern is a geometrically rationalized translation of the topology optimization.

The next stage in structural design sophistication is the methodology of topology optimization whereby the analytic capacity of FEA is turned generative by means of being looped into an evolutionary algorithm.[8] The starting point is usually a simple block shape that connects loads with support points. The FEA reveals the stress distribution under the initial conditions. Regions of low stress are then removed and the FEM is run once more on the new shape, which is then again further eroded according to the new stress distribution, and so on. The initial bounding shape to which the topology optimization algorithm is applied might itself be already a complex structurally optimized shape, like a shell form generated by the form-finding technique of mesh relaxation—as an example might here serve the experimental structure created by Zaha Hadid Architects' CODE group (Figs. 18–19).

8 X. Huang and Y.M. Xie, *Evolutionary Topology Optimization of Continuum Structures – Methods and Applications* (Chichester, United Kingdom: John Wiley & Sons Ltd., 2010).

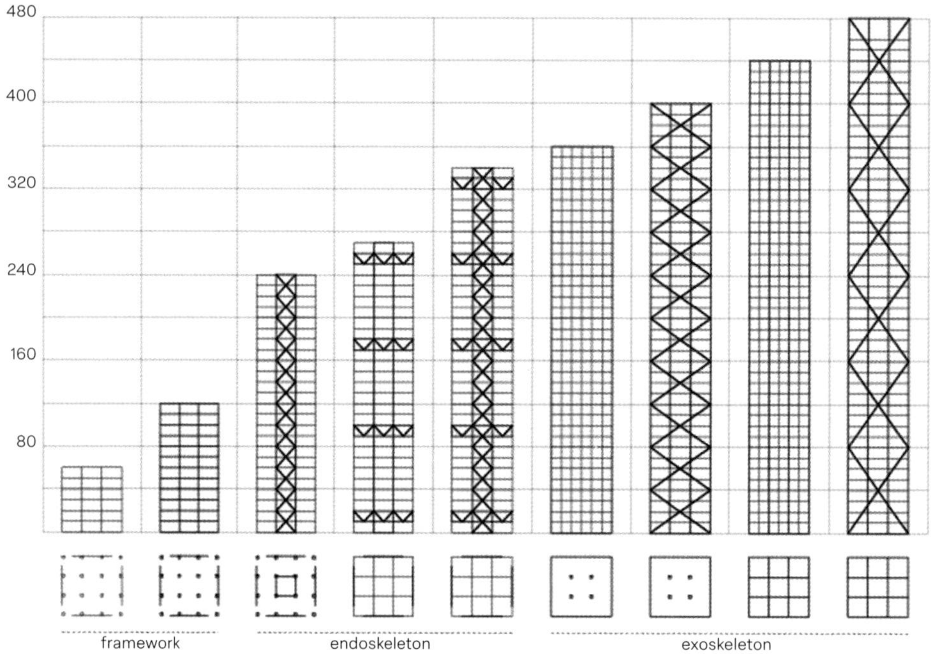

Fig. 20: These diagrams describe the modern structural principles for high-rise construction. Discrete and uniform system types—framework, endoskeleton (outrigger system), exoskeleton (structural tube system)—are selected according to a series of tower height thresholds. The underlying, unquestioned a priori stipulation or presumption here is the uniformity and discreteness of the systems.

As another recent example I would like to point to my Architectural Association's Design Research Lab (AADRL) parametric tower research (Fig. 20). The ambition here is to replace the typological structural thinking in terms of a choice from a list of structural system types, such as core-type, outrigger-type, and structural tube–type, with the idea of a tower structure that morphs across these types via a series of gradual "phase changes." Usually the tower structure is assumed to be a single, uniform system selected in accordance with the height or slenderness ratio, i.e., up to a certain height/slenderness the tower's stability can be secured by mere framing without core or bracing, while a somewhat higher tower would rely on a uniform core as stability system, while beyond this height/slenderness the outrigger system would be selected, and very tall/slender towers would be designed as a structural tube. The unquestioned presumption here is always that a tower should be conceived as a singular, uniform system without any systemic differentiation along the vertical axis of the tower. This a priori of systemic uniformity must be exposed as irrational. Its seeming rationality is the rationality of a bygone era. In former times, a topology optimized (and thus a more complex and differentiated design) was neither computable, nor buildable. However, now this default condition of system uniformity leads to a materially wasteful result.

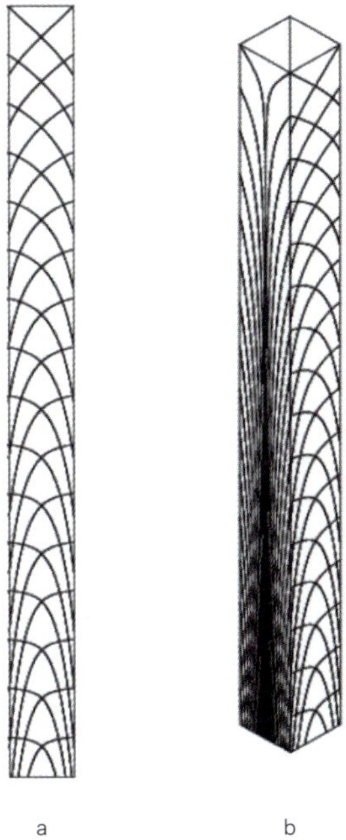

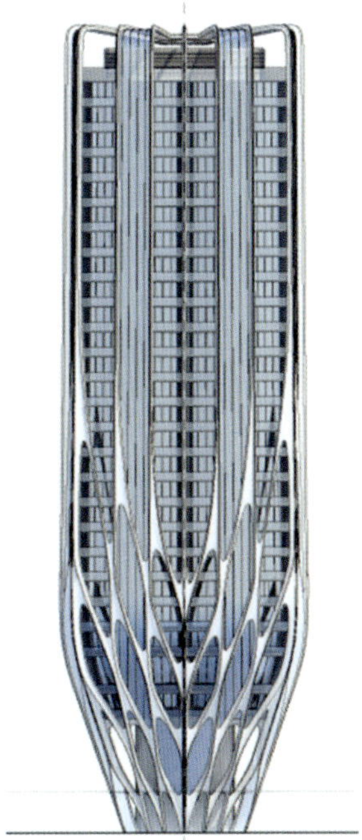

Fig. 21: Tower exoskeleton study, Studio Hadid, University of Applied Arts 2011

Fig. 22: Skeleton study for Brisbane Residential Tower, Zaha Hadid Architects 2014

The accumulation of loads and moments toward the bottom of the tower suggests that bottom, middle, and top of tower should be treated rather differently. This structural differentiation—whereby only in the lower parts of the tower the full outer surface is activated as structural tube and the upper areas might be structured rather differently—allows for a congenial programmatic differentiation. Neither programmatically, nor therefore architecturally, is uniformity any longer a desired default condition. This example once more demonstrates the congeniality of architectural parametricism and topological structural engineering.

The a priori of modern engineering rationality is thus blind to the possibility of differentiating the tower structure along its vertical axis, either by gradually varying the pattern within a given system, for instance within the exoskeleton as displayed in diagrams *a* and *b* (Fig. 21), or by shifting and blending between different systems as shown in the elevation of Zaha Hadid Architects' residential tower scheme (Fig. 22), whereby what starts as a structural tube at the bottom transforms into a simpler framework structure. The possibility of such optimizing differentiations exposes the relative irrationality (structural inefficiency) of the modern structural rationality.

Brisbane Residential Tower,
Zaha Hadid Architects 2014

3. From Engineering Inspiration to Architectural Style: Tectonism

In recent years the protagonists of parametricism have increasingly engaged themselves with design methodologies inspired by the structural form-finding techniques pioneered by Frei Otto. This is due to the availability of new digital physics engines that can simulate the material/structural form-finding methods similar to Frei Otto's experiments with physical models. These new tools, mostly available as Grasshopper plug-ins, include RhinoVAULT for complex compression-only shells, Kangaroo to approximate shell or tensile structures, or analytic tools, such as Principal Stress Lines analysis in Karamba that can also be turned generative. Even structural topology optimization tools have become readily available within the Grasshopper world. These tools deliver a quick structural form-finding capacity to designers who are now able to explore these structurally disciplined, yet still sufficiently versatile, new design worlds and are able to gain an intuitive grasp of the structural logics at play. The same also starts to happen with environmental engineering parameters, and more recently also with respect to new fabrication constraints that can be encoded within the digital design tools. Various fabrication- and materially based geometry constraints can be embedded in generative design processes that are then set free to search the characteristic solution space delimited by the constraints. At ZHA CODE (Zaha Hadid Architects' Computational Design) we are developing a lot of our own custom tools to model the constraints of particular fabrication processes.

The architects' use of these new design techniques involving engineering logics within the form-finding process does not imply that architects have become engineers, as it were re-unifying what the increasing specialization of disciplines had severed starting in the nineteenth century. Architects are designers and their use of engineering-based form-finding tools is just their way to start the collaboration with engineers on the right foot. The structural intelligence behind those tools is the intelligence of the engineering sciences, and the final structural design and liability remains exclusively the engineer's responsibility. However, the new crop of architects pose as "proto-engineers" who challenge and push the professional engineers to the frontier of their discipline, getting them involved in the new adventure of parametricism.

This new way of working has generated a new characteristic range of architectural morphologies. These morphologies are rather diverse, due to the proliferating diversity of new materials, structural approaches, and fabrication techniques. However, despite their proliferous variety, these new morphologies are recognizably of a peculiar, unmistakable cast. They share a sense of organic intricacy. This should perhaps be not too surprising after all: all these works adhere to the general principles of parametricism and furthermore share this new additional commitment to computational form finding based on engineering constraints. There is an unmistakable unity that operates across this diversity. This recognizable formal unity, together with the unity of methodological principles and values justifies the positing of a stylistic variation of parametricism: tectonism. The creations of tectonism are indeed as recognizable as the endless forms of nature are recognizable as such, namely as forms of organic nature.

Tectonism implies the stylistic heightening of engineering- and fabrication-based form-finding and optimization processes. To be clear, despite its dependency on engineering logics, "tectonism" is an *architectural* style. In fact, the concept of style(s) is a category that only makes sense within the discipline of architecture, as it necessarily refers to recognizable visual characteristics, albeit without thereby being reducible to matters of visual appearance.[9] With respect to the engineering sciences the analogous term is paradigm (rather than style). So, we can say that structural engineering's recent topological paradigm is congenial to architecture's style of parametricism, and in particular to its most recent manifestation: tectonism.

Tectonism is the most mature and potent subsidiary style (substyle) within the overarching paradigm and epochal style of parametricism. In retrospect we might distinguish tectonism from earlier phases

---

9 For a full elaboration of the concept of architectural style(s) see Patrik Schumacher, "Architectural Styles" in *The Autopoiesis of Architecture, Volume 1: A New Framework for Architecture* (London: John Wiley & Sons Ltd., 2010).

of parametricism, such as foldism and blobism.[10] In contrast to these earlier substyles tectonism is embedding a series of technical rationalities that secure both greater efficiency as well as greater morphological rigor, while maintaining sufficient degrees of design freedom to address programmatic and contextual contingencies. Since the principles that tectonism utilizes are inherently plural and open ended, this additional rigor comes along with additional tectonic variety and thereby offers a new reservoir of morphological physiognomies. This empowers designers to give a unique, recognizable identity to individual projects. Tectonism thus delivers much more expressive variety than foldism, blobism, or swarmism, without descending into arbitrary form invention.

While the overarching general design agenda remains parametricism's pursuit of adaptive differentiation, tectonism pursues these with a much richer set of parametric drivers and constraints than earlier versions of parametricism. These drivers originate in sophisticated computationally empowered engineering logics that are now available to architects at early design stages via the structural form-finding tools mentioned above.

As a substyle of parametricism, tectonism partakes in the superior social functionality of parametricism with respect to the purposes and challenges posed by our fluid contemporary societal conditions. This superiority resides in the adaptive versatility of parametricism with respect to the complex programmatic mixes that need to be intricately woven into complex urban sites. This implies complex, irregular forms, interpenetrating spaces, multiple simultaneous contextual affiliations, and gradual spatial transformations, and so on. This is what we might call spatial topology in the service of social topology.

Parametricism has the formal repertoires to shape and fit buildings so as to meet these complex requirements in ways that can also maintain legibility in the face of these unprecedented complexities. Tectonism can do all this and more: It can achieve all this while simultaneously meeting structural and environmental optimization criteria. Furthermore, the morphologies that result from this pursuit gain—as if by serendipitous coincidence—additional visual legibility advantages. How is this possible? Well, it is the very rigor of the engineering logics

10 These older substyles are still practiced, just as during the era of modernism the earlier white Bauhaus style continued in parallel with the later Brutalism.

that ruthlessly impose their selection criteria at every point across the overall form and that thus not only sponsor a formal unity across the project but also ensure that the morphological variations are rule-based and thus predictable despite their complexity.

3.1. Making Engineering Logics Speak

The demarcation between architecture and engineering[11] rests on the distinction of the built environment's *social functioning* from its *technical functioning*. While the technical functioning considers the physical integrity, fabrication constraints, and physical performance of the building in relation to its users understood as physical-biological bodies, architecture must take into consideration a building's social function. The social function of architecture is the ordering of social processes. This is achieved via spatial organization. However, buildings function only by empowering users to find their way and each other within this organization, i.e., the building must function as an ordering and guiding *communicative frame*, and is thus functioning via its appearance and *legibility*. The core competency of architecture comprises thus, besides organization, the crucial task of *articulation*. Legibility involves two aspects: the perceptual palpability and the semantic-informational charge. Accordingly, the general task of articulation bifurcates into the two specific tasks of *phenomenological articulation* and *semiological articulation*.[12] Both aspects need to guide the designer's decision-making process in the context of the proliferating options that emerge from the engineering discourse. Semiological articulation presupposes a successful phenomenological articulation. Phenomenological articulation pursues the visual decomposition of the (increasingly complex) urban scene by making the relevant functional units (units of interaction) conspicuous. This concern with the visual decomposition of a complex composition motivates us at Zaha Hadid Architects to work with curves and curved surfaces. Shells, like blobs, remain traceable spatial units even if they start clustering, intersecting, or fusing. The size of blobs or shells is communicated locally via the

---

11 Patrik Schumacher, "The Necessity of Demarcation" in *The Autopoiesis of Architecture, Volume 1: A New Framework for Architecture* (London: John Wiley & Sons Ltd., 2010).

12 Patrik Schumacher, "The Phenomenological vs. the Semiological Dimension of Architecture" in *The Autopoiesis of Architecture, Volume 2: A New Agenda for Architecture* (London: John Wiley & Sons Ltd., 2012).

Qingdao Cultural Centre, China,
Zaha Hadid Architects 2013

Figs. 23–25: Phenomenological articulation: The perceptual identification of functional units and their relations is facilitated by the use of structural shells. Convex bodies, concave spaces, and curvilinearity in general are advantageous for the visual decomposition of a complex scene. Qingdao Cultural Centre, China, Zaha Hadid Architects 2013

degree of their surface curvature. Inside versus outside is encoded as concave versus convex. Zones of overlap between such spaces clearly reveal their constitution. All these informational capacities enhance the inherent information richness and legibility of such compositions in contrast to orthogonal or cuboid systems. This is our *architectural* motivation to utilize shell structures. The structural efficiency of shell structures is of course very welcome too, and implies that we do not have to fight with our structural engineers. However, the happy coincidence between structural and architectural motivations does not imply their conflation. Our architectural reasoning proceeds as follows: The perceptual identification of functional units and their interrelations is facilitated by using convex forms like shells. The use of convex (and concave) surfaces with various degrees of curvature gives useful orienting information (Figs. 23–25). The use of structural form-finding logics disciplines the spatial morphologies in ways that are advantageous for the task of articulation, i.e., the task of elaborating a systematic spatial language.

Semiological articulation can then map significant programmatic distinctions onto conspicuous morphological distinctions so that morphological differences indicate programmatic differences. The formal unity of a structural morphology range can be perceived and help users to recognize a programmatic unity across varied instantiations. Tectonic articulation—in the style of tectonism—is thus making engineering logics speak, via a designed visual code that selects a sub-set from the set of all conceivable structural morphologies, and orchestrates these into a telling language. This language orients users as a navigation aid and tells them about the social offerings at hand. The built forms are not speaking about their structural performance (which is of no interest to users) but about their social purposes, and this communication facilitates these very purposes. Visual communication is exclusively the architect's business, not the engineer's. The engineer's business is to ensure, by means of the very same forms, their silent physical functioning. That's why the collaboration between architects and engineers must be so close and congenial: Their very different responsibilities must be met simultaneously, by the very same building forms. This collaboration between architects and engineers must become especially intensive within the style of tectonism. This style has the ambition to show, rather than to cover up and hide, the structural patterns, members, and details. These structural patterns, structural members and structural details become here articulate instruments of communication. They lead a double life, namely serving both physical-technical and cognitive-social functions.

3.2. Accentuation and Suppression

The task of articulation can be posed independently from engineering concerns as the task to orient users by means of expressive morphologies. The specific strategy of tectonic articulation as defined and proposed here is burdening the task of articulation with the constraints of engineering logics. This means that the designer's repertoire and universe of possibilities have been respectively constrained. However, contemporary engineering possibilities have recently expanded to such an extent that there remain sufficient degrees of freedom for the designer to exercise her/his core competency under the constraint of tectonic articulation. As analytic and generative computational engineering tools (physics engines) become more and more readily available to architects, they are enabled to explore this more disciplined universe of possibility with the eyes and intuitions of a designer, while simultaneously keeping engineering constraints in play. The designer can explore various engineering logics and morphologies in her/his search for a medium of articulation that allows her/him to characterize and differentiate the social functions that need to be organized and articulated. This process always involves both the visual *accentuation* of the selected morphological features as means of expression on the one hand and the visual *suppression* of all other technical features on the other hand. The raw, unedited imposition of pragmatic engineering and fabrication priorities does not deliver legibility. In fact, an unsightly visual chaos is likely to ensue, especially as there are usually multiple engineering concerns that need to be negotiated. The designer must not allow these concerns to agglomerate without aesthetic control and orchestration. Visual order needs to be imposed via a ruthless formalism and aesthetic principles that guide the accentuation and suppression of features. Tectonic articulation implies that the selected formalism has been derived from a selected engineering logic. However, the transformation of the engineering logic into a formalism is necessary to constitute tectonic articulation as architectural strategy.

Both accentuation and suppression are at play in our façade design for the Dongdaemon Design Centre in Seoul. The tessellation of the aluminum façade follows a rule (script) that converts the (smooth) differentiation of degrees of curvature into the (stepped) differentiation of degrees of subdivision. Tighter curvature leads to smaller panels. This makes sense with respect to the material fabrication constraints of sheet metal. This makes sense even though a reprogrammable mold (pin-machine) was used to press the panels into a double-curvature shape. In the areas of tighter curvature, the finer tessellation made more joints available to fit the panels to the overall curvature (Fig. 26). However, beyond this technical rationality the rule-based tessellation strategy delivers a heightened visual plasticity and thus legibility of the buildings form. The turning points in the surface are being accentuated by the denser tessellation.

Fig. 26: The tessellation follows a rule that correlates curvature with subdivision. This makes sense in terms of fabrication. This also is a strategy of phenomenological articulation: it accentuates the plastic features of the form and thus enhances its perceptual palpability. Dongdaemon Design Centre, Seoul, Korea, Zaha Hadid Architects 2007–2014

The volume's shape becomes perceptually more palpable, also from the distance and under less favorable lighting conditions. The second plasticity-enhancing detailing strategy is the utilization of iso-curves as tessellation lines. These curves follow and thus accentuate the flow of the surface rather than being arbitrarily imposed onto the surface.

Suppression is also at work here. The major spaces of the design center do not need any daylight. Therefore, an altogether solid façade is an appropriate response. However, there are various ancillary spaces that do require windows. Rather than allowing these windows to disrupt the fluidity of the overall form we decided to radically suppress the existence of these windows by letting the smooth envelope

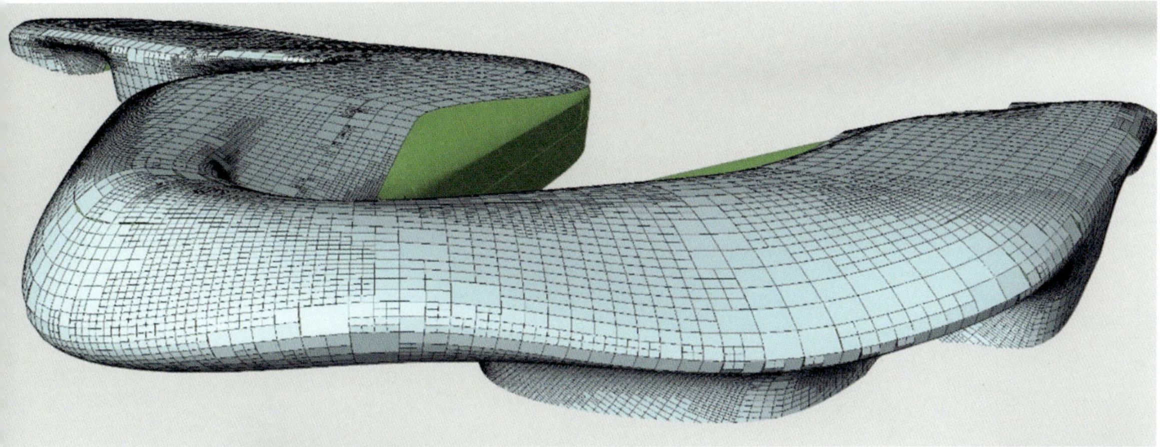

Figs. 27–28: Accentuation and suppression: subdivisions and joints follow and accentuate the surface curvature. Perforations suppress the expression of windows and allow for the monolithic sculptural expression of the overall complex volume. Dongdaemon Design Centre, Seoul, Korea, Zaha Hadid Architects 2007–2014

Dongdaemon Design Centre plaza and park,
Seoul, Korea, Zaha Hadid Architects 2007–2014

continue uninterrupted across these windows. The need for light was accommodated by perforating the metal sheets that hide the windows. Moreover, the location of the windows is being further dissimulated by avoiding any one-to-one correlations between windows and perforated panels. Instead, the distribution of the perforated panels across the façade has been to some extent randomized, thus adding to the overall organic expression of the building (Figs. 27–28). The windows would have disrupted the architectural figure and would have drawn more attention to themselves than their functions merits. Cuts within the envelope have been reserved for the entrances, which are thus as conspicuously communicated as one could wish. Legibility in the service of quick, intuitive orientation and navigation—prerequisites of the building's social functionality—are the accomplishments of these strategies of tectonic articulation.

3.3. Tectonic Articulation

The relationship between the technical and the articulatory dimension of the built environment leads to the general concept of tectonics, here understood as the architectural selection and utilization of technically motivated engineered forms and details for the sake of an articulation that aims at legibility for the sake of social communication.

Tectonic articulation is here thus proposed as the concept for the strategic articulatory utilization of the morphological differentiations that emerge from engineering logics, such as structural engineering, environmental engineering, and façade engineering.

The history of architecture abounds with examples where architectural elements and features with technical functions become the object of articulatory or "ornamental" endeavors. However, we need to understand the instrumentality of ornament, i.e., we need to grasp ornament not in contrast to performance but as a special type of performance: communicative performance. A technically efficient morphology thus assumes also an articulatory, communicative function.

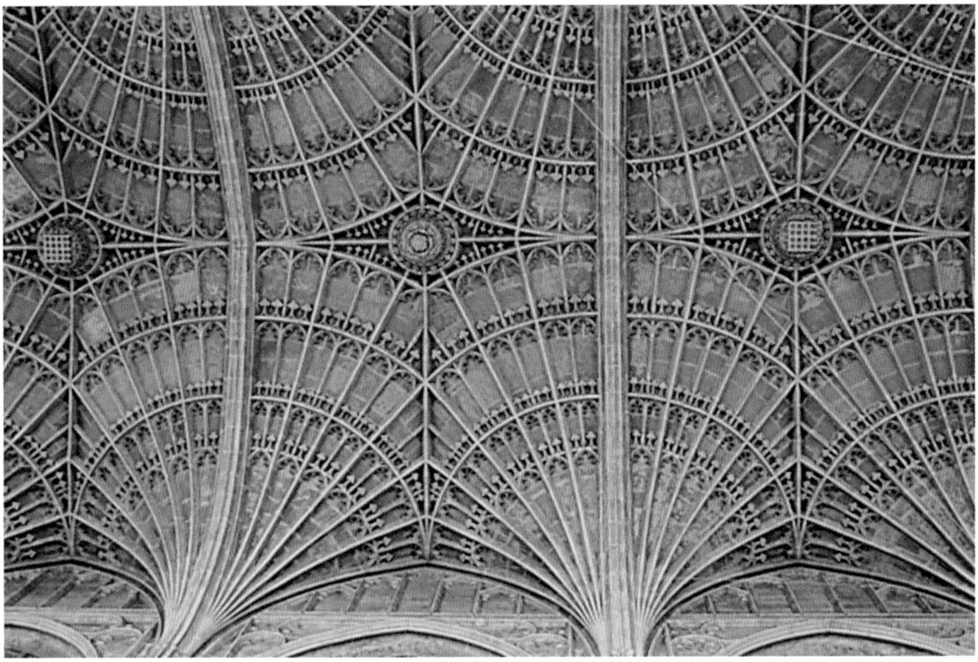

Fig. 29: Gothic-style fan vault, King's College Chapel, Cambridge, United Kingdom 1446–1515

The variety and expressiveness of Gothic vaults clearly build upon structurally motivated patterns, and clearly heighten these patterns into an ornamental expressive state that communicates the special purpose and dignity of the space (Fig. 29). These spaces are thus examples of what we are theorizing here as tectonic articulation. Zaha Hadid Architects has been trying to emulate and further enhance this expressive-ornamental exploitation of structural patterns for the purposes of semiological articulation, for instance with the design of the Presidential Palace in Algiers (Figs. 30–32). This project is further explained in the chapter on structural logics (see 4.2. Structural System Optimizations as Drivers of Tectonic Articulation, page 73).

It is one of the key theses of my general theory of architecture that semiological articulation is the latent function of all investments into ornament, and that semiological articulation is a key contribution to the social functionality of the built environment. The exploitation of synergies between structural and semiological or communicative functionality lies at the heart of the paradigm and style of tectonism.

Figs. 30–32: Presidential Palace, Algiers, Algeria, Zaha Hadid Architects 2011–2017

The articulatory integration of the morphological consequences of technical requirements is always the more elegant solution than the attempt to fight and deny them by hiding or obfuscating them. This latter stance would require the invention of additional communicative features because social distinctions desire and require expression. However, the utilization of the initially technically motivated morphological features for the characterization of spaces is not only more economical but leads to a higher level of credibility of the communication because the morphological signifier is already an index rather than a merely arbitrary symbol.

Thus, in the terminology of Charles Sanders Peirce (1839–1914), tectonic articulation transforms "indexical signs" into "symbolic signs." This process, too, gives degrees of freedom to the designer in the selection of the indexical features that might be heightened and systematized to become elements of a semiological system of signification.[13] In order for architects to pursue tectonic articulation they need to guide and orchestrate the engineering investigations and then select the engineering options that most suit their primary task, namely to fulfill the posed social functions via framing spatio-morphological communications. The adaptive differentiation of load-bearing structures as well as the adaptive differentiation of volumes and envelopes according to the building's environmental performance (with respect to its exposure to sun, wind, rain, and so on) as well as differentiations that stem from fabrication logics (e.g., tessellations) afford many opportunities for differential tectonic articulation. A thus lawfully differentiated built environment would be much more legible and navigable than the modernist, isotropic order of repetition. With the development of sophisticated computational design tools—both within architecture, within the engineering disciplines, and within the construction industry—the scope for nuanced tectonic articulation has much increased. The adaptation of structural morphologies to the force distribution within a structural system offers a fantastic opportunity for architectural articulation. In turn the more complex architectural orders proposed within contemporary architecture are reflected and potentially accentuated by sophisticated, adaptive structures. The realization of this potential requires an intensified collaboration between innovative architects, engineers, and fabricators. Although there can be no doubt that architecture remains a discourse that is distinct from engineering and construction, a close collaboration with these disciplines as well as the acquisition of reliable intuitions about their respective logics are increasingly important conditions for the design of contemporary high-performance environments. These environments will no longer be based on a typology of fixed stereotypes. These environments will be topological environments: socially, spatially, and structurally.

---

13 A certain drawback here is that the articulatory repertoire is thereby somewhat constrained, so that this strategy might not succeed if the task of articulation is very complex.

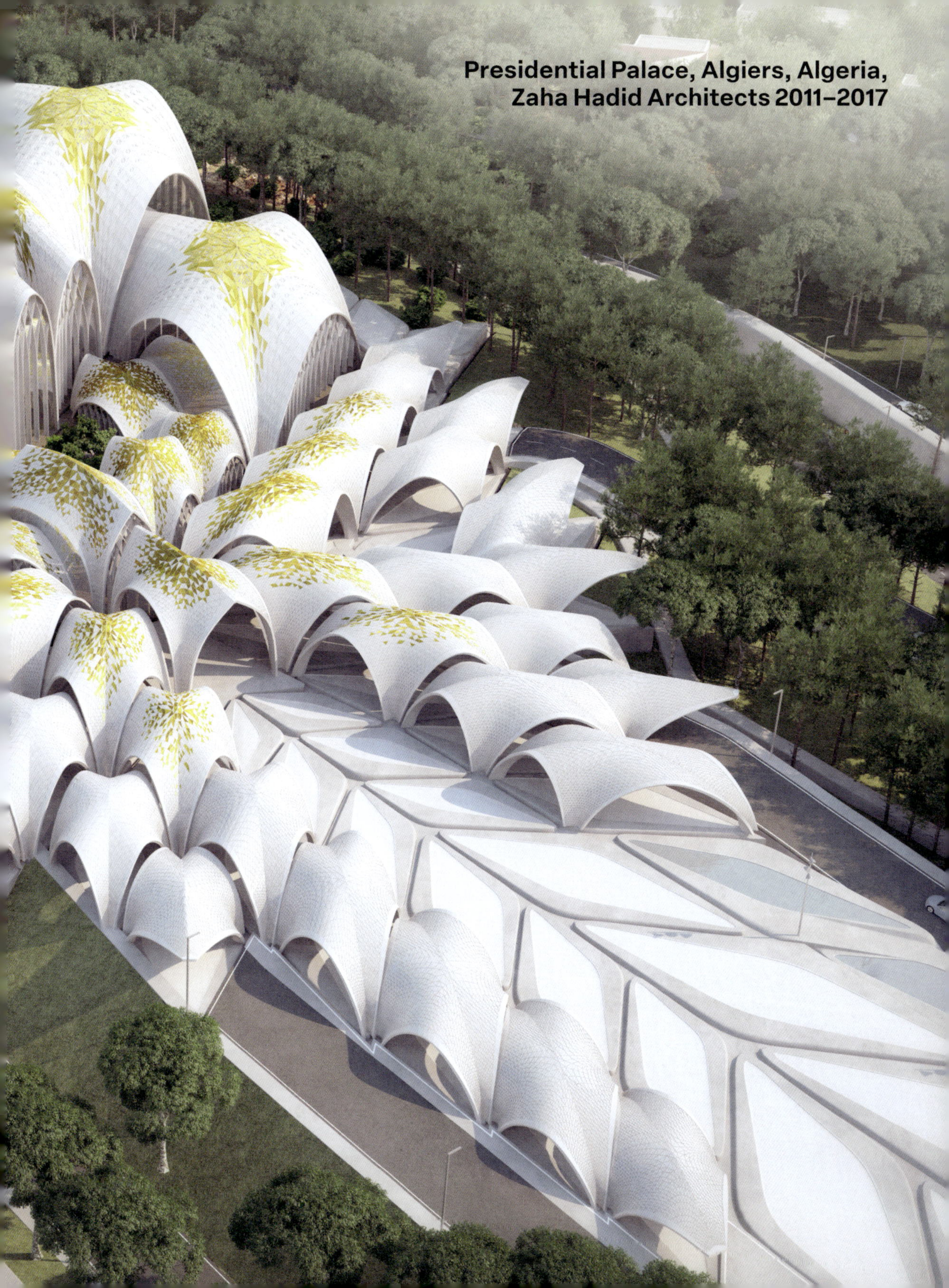

Presidential Palace, Algiers, Algeria,
Zaha Hadid Architects 2011–2017

4. Tectonism as Style: Expressive Utilization of Engineering Logics

Recent advances in computationally empowered engineering tools and advances in numerically controlled fabrication technologies increasingly feed back into the formal repertoires prevalent in avant-garde architectural design, product design, and even fashion design. This feedback is actively and strategically pursued by the current protagonists of parametricism who are experimenting with the new digital design and fabrication technologies, not so much to empower their prior design sensibilities and intentions but to discover new sensibilities and repertoires in the new rather particular sets of affordances and constraints that come with the different fabrication technologies explored.

On the basis of industrial robots as generic fabrication infrastructure, the specific technologies and end effectors are explored and developed within the experimental architectural studios themselves—mostly within and around schools of architecture—rather than being delivered ready-made from outside. While the manifest explicit agenda is the rational utilization of the new productivity-enhancing technologies, i.e., the designers are manifestly invested in technical functionality, this book argues that the latent, implicit agenda is the expansion of architecture's design repertoire and morphology, i.e., the elaboration of a new style. The pragmatic promise of fabrication efficiency is an attractive premise for designers but it is not the most important motivation here: what really attracts designers to the new technologies is their promise of new creative and expressive powers.

We indeed witness an intensive new investment in architecture's stylistic resources. We are witnessing the formation of a new style: *tectonism*. *Tectonism* implies the stylistic heightening of engineering- and fabrication-based form-finding and optimization processes.

However, this style does not spell a departure from parametricism. Rather, tectonism is the currently most prevalent and promising *subsidiary style* (substyle) within the overarching paradigm and epochal style of parametricism. In retrospect we might distinguish tectonism from earlier phases of parmetricism like foldism (Fig. 33), blobism (Fig. 34), and swarmism (Fig. 35).[14] In comparison to these earlier substyles tectonism maintains sufficient degrees of design freedom while embedding a series of technical rationalities that secure both greater efficiency as well as greater morphological rigor. Since the design principles tectonism utilizes are inherently plural and open ended, this additional rigor delivers additional variety and thereby a new reservoir of morphological physiognomies that can help to give a unique, recognizable identity to individual projects without relying on formal invention.

While the overarching general design agenda remains parametricism's pursuit of adaptive versatility and complexity, tectonism pursues these agendas with a much richer set of parametric drivers and constraints than earlier versions of parametricism. These drivers originate in sophisticated computationally empowered engineering logics that are now available to architects at early design stages via structural form-finding tools like RhinoVAULT (for complex compression-only shells) and physics engines like Kangaroo plug-ins for Grasshopper (to approximate shell or tensile structures), via analytic tools like Principal Stress Lines analysis in Karamba that can also be turned generative, and via optimization tools, such as structural topology optimization (e.g., in Millipede, Ameba, Peregrine, "tOpos," or Altair's Optistruct). At ZHA CODE we are programming our own tools to allow designers to form-find geometric solutions that are informed by fabrication processes like curved-crease folding with metal sheets, or the assembly of compression-only shells from 3D printed concrete segments. This enables the intuitive engagement with fabrication and material constraints.

All this leads to uniquely characteristic morphologies and features that nevertheless all remain recognizable as variants of tectonism and indeed parametricism because all these techniques follow the overarching methodology of parametricism favoring parametric malleability. In earlier writings I had identified Frei Otto as the only true precursor of parametricism. This identification and honor also applies in relation to tectonism: Frei Otto and the legacy of his research institute are a huge inspiration to the protagonists of tectonism.

---

14 Foldism, blobism, and swarmism emerged in quick succession in the 1990s and merged. Tectonism is upgrading rather than merely varying parametricism.

Fig. 33 (top left): Foldism, here. Guangzhou Opera House, Guangzhou, China, Zaha Hadid Architects 2003–201

Fig. 34 (top right): Blobism, here. Galaxy SOHO, Beijing, China, Zaha Hadid Architect 2009–2012

Fig. 35 (bottom left): Swarmism, here. Hoenheim-Nord Terminus, Strasbourg France, Zaha Hadid Architects 1998–200

Fig. 36 (bottom right) Tectonism, here. King Abdullah Petroleum Studies & Research Centre (KAPSARC), Riyadh, Saudi Arabia, Zaha Hadid Architects 2009–2017

It is important to note that tectonism—like the earlier stages within parametricism—is already operating across all design disciplines, although architecture remains its heartland.

Many of the best current protagonists of parametricism might be classified as belonging to tectonism as defined here: Achim Menges, Marc Fornes, Fabio Gramazio and Matthias Kohler, Philippe Block, Philip Yuan, and Mark Burry among many others. Some of the recent work of Zaha Hadid Architects where structural and environmental engineering logics as well as fabrication logics play an increasingly formative role in the morphology and tectonic articulation of the design can also be classified as tectonism, in particular the various experimental installations developed within ZHA CODE, but also projects like the Serpentine Gallery (Figs. 50–51), the One Thousand Museum tower (page 94), the recently completed King Abdullah Petroleum Studies & Research Center (Fig. 36; see also page 104), as well as various projects in planning at the moment: projects using reticulated concrete shells, tensile structures, exoskeletons, articulated timber structures, and so on. Further we can include some of Nike's best products, such as its Firefly shoes, or some of ODLO's best sportswear. Here fabric tailoring and unusual knitting textures are driven by engineering concerns, such as temperature management, moisture management, and movement management via various directions and degrees of elasticity, with gradient ribbing and perforation patterns, and so on. These innovations and their aesthetic expression inspired my own forays into fashion design.

4.1. Historical Precedents

While Frei Otto (1925–2015) was the only true precursor of parametricism, and indeed of tectonism, there were other important precedents, such as Antoni Gaudí (1852–1926) and Félix Candela (1910–1997), who also played a role in the architectural discourse of parametricism and tectonism. Gaudí was a radical innovator with his inventive use of complex geometry, such as conic and ruled surfaces. For his masterpiece, the cathedral La Sagrada Familia in Barcelona (Figs. 37–38), he used hyperboloids to define the shape of the vaults, an unprecedented move. The columns carrying the vaults are also unique: they branch and tilt. This in turn implies that no buttresses were required on the outside of the nave.

La Sagrada Familia was left unfinished at Gaudí's death and was initially continued by his disciples and later by a board of expert engineers and architects. One of these architects in charge was the New Zealand native/Australian architect Mark Burry who became an influential contributor to the development of parametricism and tectonism.

Figs. 37–38: La Sagrada Familia by Antoni Gaudí, Barcelona, Spain (ongoing since 1882)

Even more noteworthy and influential than La Sagrada Familia was Gaudí's method of hanging chain models to define the geometry of vaults. The hanging models lead to catenary curves. Catenary curves equalize the tension in a rope, cable, or chain under self-weight. In Gaudí's time they had been used only for suspension bridges. Gaudí introduced this curve into masonry architecture by flipping the hanging curves to give an arching shape now optimized for compression. Gaudí developed this method of hanging models to model the forms of a complex network of such catenary arches. He used this method for the unfinished Church of Colònia Güell (Fig. 39). What is remarkable here (as with La Sagrada Familia) is the use of non-classical complex geometries that could deliver an increased level of structural efficiency. However, this radically non-traditional approach is not very conspicuous and somehow hidden due to the traditional global form of the basilica type and due to the material and ornamentation of these structures. Gaudí's unique work belongs to no identifiable style. It has however been classified as part of art nouveau. This style was rather short lived as a transitional style between nineteenth-century historicism and twentieth-century modernism.

Fig. 39: Hanging inverse structural model by Antoni Gaudí, Church of Colònia Güell, Barcelona, Spain, circa 1900

The geometry of hyperbolic paraboloids (hypars) was later used as a global building form to dramatic effect by the modernist Spanish/Mexican engineer and architect Félix Candela (1910–1997). Candela designed, engineered, and built—doubling as contractor—many efficient concrete shell structures that were very cost effective due to the structural efficiency of the double-curved shell forms (Figs. 40–44). Candela's constructions were therefore highly competitive solutions also for industrial buildings. The inherent graceful elegance of these complex but rigorously formed structures also implied their suitability

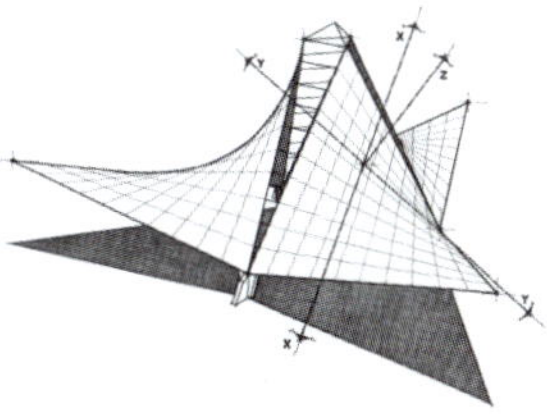

Fig. 40: Bacardi rum factory by Félix Candela, Tultitlán de Mariano Escobedo, Mexico 1960

Figs. 41–44: Capella San Vicente de Paul by Félix Candela, Mexico City, Mexico 1959

for churches. Industrial halls and churches are thus the primary users of Candela's shells. The global non-traditional form and the pure execution without ornament aligns these works with modernism, especially as simple plan geometries, modularity, and symmetries are maintained.

A more radical departure from all traditional architectural preconceptions was achieved by the German architect and engineer Frei Otto (1925–2015), the only full-blown precursor of parametricism and tectonism.

Fig. 45: Cable-net structure by Frei Otto, German Exhibition Pavilion, Expo '67, Montreal, Canada 196

Fig. 46: Cable-net structure by Frei Otto, Olympic Stadium, Munich, Germany 197

Gaudí's method of the catenary hanging model was radicalized and generalized by Frei Otto's principle of "form finding" as the paradigm for an expansive research program using analogies with natural formations and physically pliable models in the pursuit of innovative lightweight structures. In order to systematically pursue his research agenda, Frei Otto founded the Institute for Lightweight Structures in 1964, at the University of Stuttgart. (I was a student at the university from 1983 to 1987 benefitting from Frie Otto's teaching.) The results of Frei Otto's research were extraordinary and path breaking. The whole canon of classical and modern architecture was left behind and something radically novel emerged, wholly unprecedented in its open-ended proliferation of complex forms, untethered from any traditional notion of architectural type and order (Figs. 45–48). However, to describe these architectural forms as "free-form" would not be appropriate because these forms are rigorously determined by structural optimization processes. Later, within the parametricism discourse, Frei Otto's method was characterized as "material computing."

The more our design research and work evolved on the basis of algorithmic form generation, the more we learned to appreciate the work of pioneers like Frei Otto who had achieved the most elegant designs on the basis of material-structural form-finding processes. From Frei Otto we learned how the richness, organic coherence and fluidity of the forms and spaces we desire could emerge rationally from an intricate balance of forces. We expanded Frei Otto's method to include environmental as well as structural logics, and we moved from material computation to digital simulations, thereby vastly expanding our explorative search capacity.

Figs. 47–49: Lightweight timber grid shell by Frei Otto, Multihalle, Mannheim, Germany 1975

4.2. Structural System Optimizations as Drivers of Tectonic Articulation

The exposure of the primary structure can be very effective in giving an identifiable character and atmosphere to the different spaces within a building. The orchestration of the engineering and design agendas might succeed as follows: The design process might proceed in the following sequencing of concerns—spatial ordering, technical performance/materialization, articulation. (It is only the second concern—the technical performance/materialization—where engineering input must be integrated.) The materialized organization (materialized according to the concerns of technical efficiency) produces a certain morphology with a certain appearance. Before adding an additional material layer for the purposes of articulation, it thus makes sense to investigate whether this technically given material morphology is suited to serve the required articulatory function. The recent ability of computationally based structural engineering techniques to offer parametric variation and nuanced parametric differentiations of structural systems is congenial with the rule-based approach and the general aesthetic principles of the contemporary style of parametricism. The structural engineering logic of adapting member sizes in proportion to stresses can be taken up within an architectural strategy of articulation. The internal ordering of large spaces might be facilitated by the lawful differentiation of the structural system: the different (longitudinal versus transversal) directions of the space might be indicated by the direction of the primary beams. The center of a large space might be indicated by the greatest depth of the beams, and so on. These features might serve as orienting clues within a large, otherwise visually partitioned space like a large market space. Another example might be the case of a skeleton of a tower that is being expressed on the outside as an exoskeleton. It might be differentiated along the vertical axis describing a gradient transformation from massive to filigree. This structural logic might be visually accentuated to become perceptually palpable and systematically correlated with an occupational logic so that the structure's articulation might in turn come to signify the occupational distribution. Thus the sequences of structural changes from massive to filigree might come to signify the programmatic stacking from retail (massive) via workspaces, to residential spaces (filigree). A simpler alignment of the structural differentiation of a tower exoskeleton with its programmatic differentiation has been achieved in our design for a residential tower in Miami (see One Thousand Museum, page 94). Here the skeleton thins out from the three-bay structure at the lower part of the tower via a two-bay structure in the middle section to become a single-bay structure at the top of the tower. This structural transformation is correlated with the division of the floor plates into three apartments in the lower part, two apartments per floor in the middle section, and single penthouse-style apartments at the top segment of the tower. Through this correspondence the exoskeleton thus expresses the differentiation and distribution of the program (apartment types) within the tower.

Figs. 50–51: Lilas, temporary tensile fabric installation, Serpentine Gallery, London, United Kingdom, Zaha Hadid Architects 2007

The general principles of the new computationally empowered structural engineering methods and the purposes of structurally informed tectonic articulation have been outlined and argued for above. This chapter introduces a small number of illustrative examples from the oeuvre of Zaha Hadid Architects that also allow us to refer to several specific structural principles and related tools. The first sequence of projects are tensile structures inspired by the work of Frei Otto. However, the use of high pylons is explicitly avoided in our tensile projects.

The Lilas installation for the Serpentine Gallery's annual summer party consisted of three identical, asymmetric tensile fabric structures, arranged like parasols around the center of the space (Figs. 50–51). The piece was inspired by the complex natural geometry of flower petals and leaves. Each widened gracefully from a slender base into a broad, cantilevered canopy more than sixteen feet (five meters) high. The three parasols overlapped without touching (mediating between open and closed spaces), allowing air, light, and sound to travel freely. The Lilas were elevated on a low platform in the center of the site. During the day, its canopy provided shade; at night it was transformed into a light reflector for the light that radiated from the base. The light highlighted the fabric seams that follow the logic of tailoring that gives the fabric its three-dimensional anticlastic form. These illuminated bands gave the impression of veins, revealing the geometric intricacy of the Lilas and tracing the delicate curve of the forms.

Figs. 52–55: The Serpentine North Gallery, Hyde Park, London, United Kingdom, Zaha Hadid Architects 2009–2013

The Lilas project led to the commission of the Serpentine North Gallery. The Serpentine North Gallery (Figs. 52–55) consists of two distinct parts, namely the conversion of a classical nineteenth-century brick structure—The Magazine—and a twenty-first-century tensile structure. The brick structure was transformed into the gallery space while the tensile structure serves as a connected social space. The structure balances three systems, a continuous steel tube that describes a series of three-dimensional arches tilting outward, a tensile membrane stretched between these arches, and a system of columns pushing the tensile membrane upward. These columns double as light wells as they open up at the top. This also avoids load concentrations by substituting a loop for a point. The overall surface geometry and thus the global morphology of the building is determined as a characteristic anticlastic, minimal tension surface that follows the logic of tensile force equilibration and minimization.

The Mathematics Gallery at the Science Museum in London (Fig. 56) is the third tensile structure we constructed in London. It has a complex floating minimal surface. The gallery brings together remarkable stories, historical artifacts, and design to highlight the central role of mathematical practice in all our lives, and explores how mathematicians, their tools, and ideas have helped build the modern world over the past four centuries, from the Renaissance to the present day. The hanging, looping structure partitions the overall space into various zones within the exhibition space while touching neither ground nor ceiling, and without altogether screening off the spaces visually from each other. Glimpses and deeply layered vistas are afforded, and shift depending on whether visitors stand or sit. Sitting down affords more visual penetration.

The exploration of shell and tensile structures, and especially the combination of hard shells and soft tensile surfaces in a single structure, had been a design research theme in my various teaching arenas, such as at the Architectural Association's Design Research Lab (AADRL), the Hadid Masterclass at the University of Applied Arts in Vienna, as well as at Harvard Graduate School of Design. The results of the Vienna masterclass were displayed at the Venice Architecture Biennale in 2012. An early instance of the research at

Fig. 56: Mathematics Gallery, Science Museum, London, United Kingdom, Zaha Hadid Architects 2014–2016

Mathematics Gallery, Science Museum, London, United Kingdom, Zaha Hadid Architects 2014–2016

the AADRL is illustrated in Figs. 57–61. The Inside-out Parametric Gothic project took inspiration from Gothic basilica vaults with ribs bundling into cluster columns. The design aims to deliver the structural expression as much on the outside as on the inside, in contrast to the mainly internal articulation of the Gothic vaults. Instead of the traditional repetitive series of bays, this project operates with a gradual parametric variation of bays as well as a bifurcation and layering of naves. Instead of only working with compression shells, the project combines arches and vaults working in compression with tensile elements. Finally, the profiles of all linear members are subject to continuous adaptive variation. The curved plan geometry follows the overall pliant fitting of the building into its site. These remarkable intricacies are beautifully resolved with a sense of effortless elegance.

Figs. 57–61: Inside-ou Parametric Gothic, AADRL 2010 (team: Maria Tsironi, Gerry Cruz, Natalie Popik, Spyridon Kaprinis)

Figs. 62–63: Winning competition entry for the Tokyo 2020 Olympic Stadium, Japan, Zaha Hadid Architects 2014

Our winning competition design of the main stadium for the Tokyo 2020 Olympic Games (Figs. 62–63) was developed as a combination of shell and tensile structures, with a big skeletal shell or a system of linked arches filled in with cable-net surfaces. The geometry thus combines hard, opaque, and synclastic with soft, translucent, anticlastic surfaces, with tangential surface continuity across both categories.

As protagonists of concrete shell construction like Félix Candela and Heinz Isler had demonstrated, concrete shells can deliver efficient large-span spaces. Zaha Hadid Architects' extensive studies for the Presidential Palace in Algiers utilize optimized shell morphologies (Fig. 64) as well as structural reticulation patterns (Figs. 65–66) to articulate a grouping of a wide variety of spaces (Figs. 67–73).

Fig. 64: Optimized shell morphologies, Presidential Palace, Algiers, Algeria, Zaha Hadid Architects 2011–2017

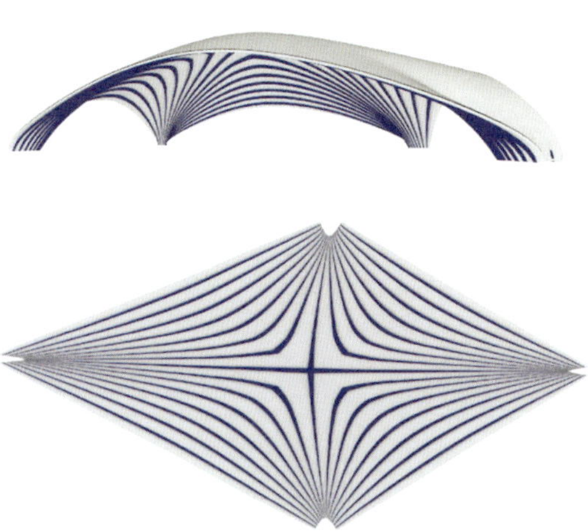

Figs. 65–66: Structur reticulation patterns, Presidential Palace, Algiers, Algeria, Zaha Hadid Architects 2011–2017

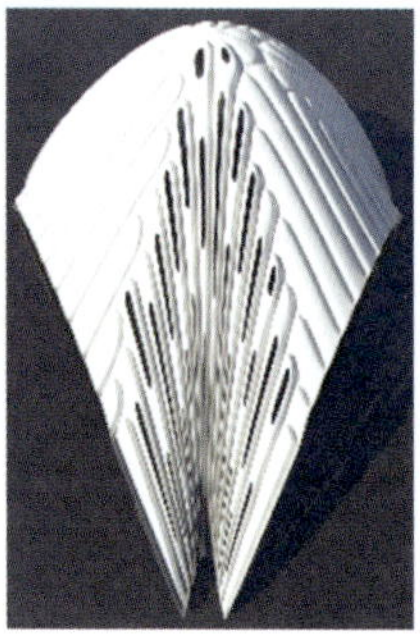

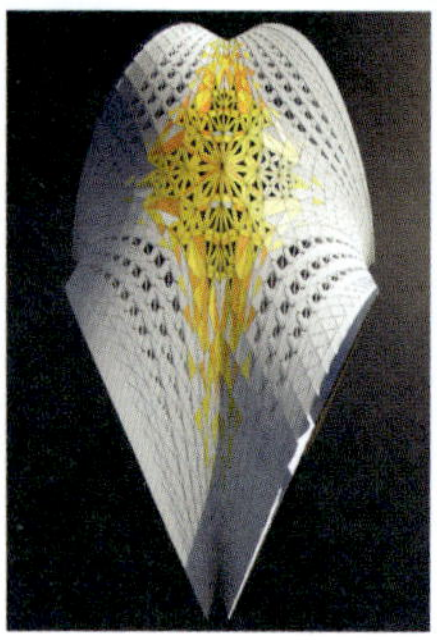

Figs. 67–73: Structura reticulation patterns, Presidential Palace, Algiers, Algeria, Zaha Hadid Architects 2011–2017

Figs. 74–76: External shell forms, internal ribbing, and perforation patterns, Presidential Palace, Algiers, Algeria, Zaha Hadid Architects 2011–2017

Both the external shell forms as well as the internal ribbing and perforation patterns are based on structural optimization algorithms. There are many ways to set up and compute the structural optimization, and many more ways to translate these abstract force flow patterns into a tectonic order of profiles and reticulated surfaces. Thus, this design method delivers a rich variety of articulations that can then be instrumentalized for the expressive semiological articulation and characterization of the various spaces like central entry lobbies, grand ballroom, and so on (Figs. 74–76). Some of the ribbing patterns also function as internal orientation lines indicating primary entry points and spatial center points.

Fig. 77: Armadillo Vau by Block Research Group, Venice Architecture Biennale Venice, Italy 2016

The outstanding contemporary champion of innovative parametric compression vaults is Philippe Block with his research group at ETH Zürich. One of his most spectacular feats is the Armadillo Vault (Fig. 77) presented at the Venice Architecture Biennale in 2016. Zaha Hadid Architects had invited him four years earlier to participate in our display at the Venice Architecture Biennale in 2012 where he showed some of his models. In the interim he had developed RhinoVAULT, his sophisticated graphic statics-based 3D design engine to optimize compression-only shells without relying on any symmetry assumption in his equilibrations, thereby bringing stone vaults into the domain of parametric design, with unheard of degrees of design freedom, yet guaranteeing structural integrity and tectonic rigor. About the Armadillo Vault the Block Research Group states: "Comprising 399 individually cut limestone pieces, unreinforced and assembled without mortar, the Armadillo Vault spans fifty-two feet (sixteen meters) with a minimum thickness of only two inches (five centimeters). Its funicular geometry allows it to stand in pure compression, while tension ties equilibrate the form. Starting from the same structural and constructional principles as historic stone cathedrals, this sophisticated form emerged from novel computational graphic statics-based design and optimization methods developed by the project team."

The characterful morphological and tectonic articulation, from global form down to the detail, including the incredible differential thickness/thinness, the tessellation patterns, the surface rifts that result from leaving the stones flat on top, and the stone grooving texture on the underside, makes this project a paradigmatic example of tectonism at its best.

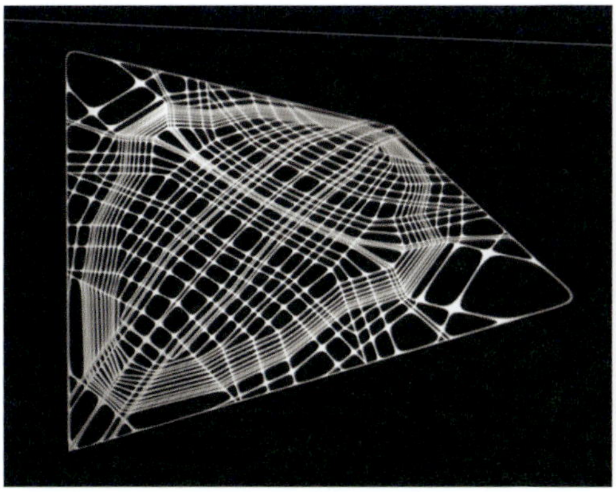

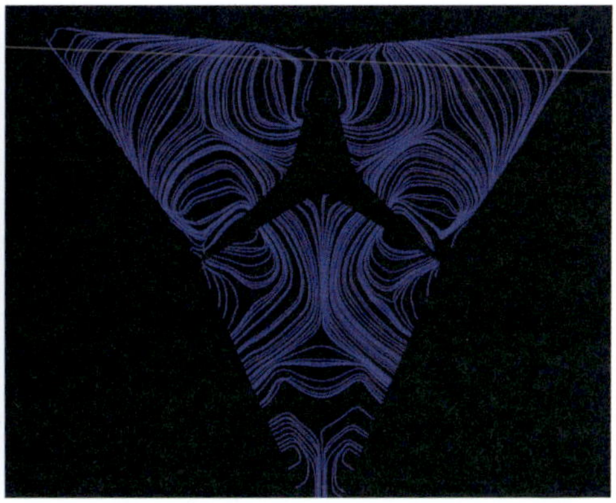

Figs. 78–79: Primary stress lines inscribed and extruded onto a hypar shell form, ZHA CODE

Candela Revisited

Pavilion for the China International Architectural Biennale, Beijing, China 2013, Zaha Hadid Architects

In 2013 the Beijing, China Architectural Biennale called for ideas to reactivate the post-Olympic urban space between Beijing's Bird's Nest and Water Cube. For Zaha Hadid Architects, this was an opportunity to create an open pavilion space that could frame social interaction within the vast area of the Olympic site with a graceful, light structure that can demonstrate our new interest in structural articulation based on computationally supported optimization.

Figs. 80–81: Candela Revisited, ZHA CODE with Bollinger-Grohmann, China International Architectural Biennale, Beijing, China 2013

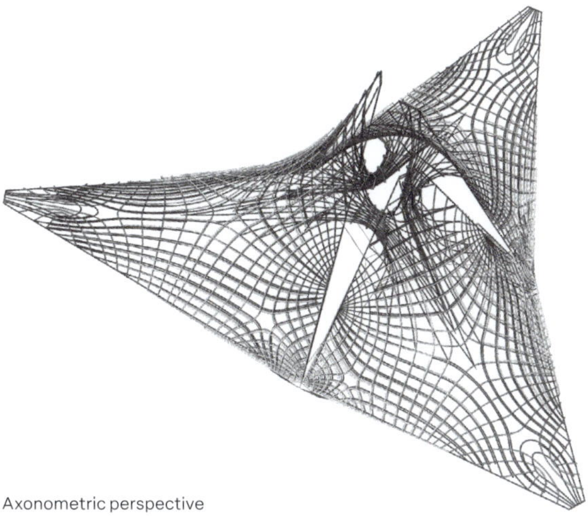

Axonometric perspective

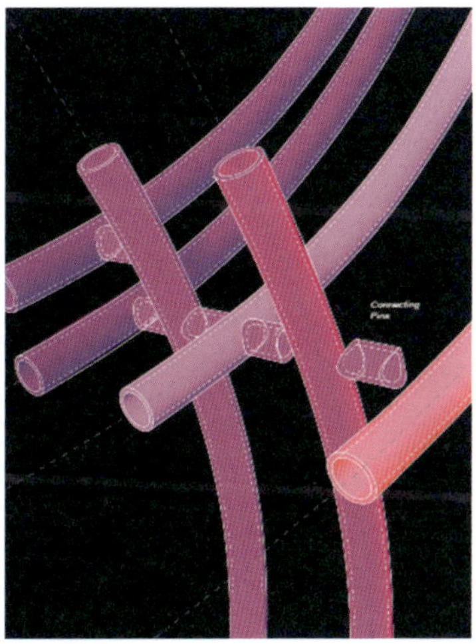

Figs. 82–83: Candela Revisited, Zaha Hadid Architects/ ZHA CODE with Bollinger-Grohmann, experimental pavilion, China International Architectural Biennale Beijing, China 2013

The pavilion provided us with the opportunity to continue our research into articulated shell structures with a built prototype. The structure is following a historical lineage of design research within the domain of physical form-finding, such as hanging chains, soap films, et al., pioneered by the likes of Antoni Gaudí, Heinz Isler, Frei Otto, Félix Candela, and others. The pavilion for the China International Architectural Biennale as a research-prototype aims to extend this work to adequately represent our ambitions in digital design systems and delivery mechanisms. The project explores synergies between architectural articulation, engineering logic, and fabrication constraints. It continues Zaha Hadid Architects' ongoing research on the architectural articulation of self-supporting, thin, curved surface geometries. The more our design research and work evolves on the basis of algorithmic form generation, the more we learn to appreciate the work of pioneers like Félix Candela, who had achieved the most elegant designs on the basis of material and structural form-finding processes.

It was a natural point to start our research where the grand masters had finished theirs. Félix Candela's Capella San Vicente de Paul in Mexico City[15] provided exactly the right spatial setting: three hyperbolic paraboloids opening up in all directions. Like Félix Candela's building, our structure comprises three hyperbolic paraboloids with their tips meeting high in the air. Our take works with a broken rather than perfect symmetry. In contrast to Candela's smooth shell, our shell is a layered grid shell whereby the reticulation pattern follows the Principal Stress Lines analyzed via the structural analysis software Karamba (Figs. 78–79).

15 Ballard Metcalfe, "A Structural Optimization of Félix Candela's Chapel of St. Vincent de Paul in Coyoacán, Mexico City," (United States: Princeton University Undergraduate Senior Theses, Civil and Environmental Engineering, 2014).

Figs. 84–85: KnitCandela. Zaha Hadid Architects' computation and design research group (ZHA CODE) collaborated with ETH ürich's Block Research Group to design and manufacture the KnitCrete formwork system.

Stress densities were translated approximately via the number of grid-line layers: one, two, or three layers. These stress lines are more efficient and more beautiful than the imposition of a generic grid could have been. The grid shell has been constructed from very slender steel tubes, joined via spacers rather than letting them intersect or touch (Figs. 80–81). As stresses build up toward the support points we added additional layers of steel tubes. The system was visually further articulated via the differential coloring of the layers, thereby further accentuating the intricacy of the structure (Figs. 82–83).

KnitCandela is our second experimental structure that pays homage to the Spanish-Mexican architect and engineer Félix Candela. KnitCandela (Figs. 84–85) reimagines his inventive concrete shell structures through the introduction of new computational design methods and innovative KnitCrete formwork technology. KnitCandela's form references Candela's acclaimed Los Manantiales restaurant pavilion at Xochimilco, Mexico City; a concept he further developed in several of his subsequent projects. While Candela relied on combining hyperbolic paraboloid surfaces (hypars) to produce reusable formworks leading to a reduction of construction waste, KnitCrete allows for the realization of a much wider range of anticlastic geometries. With this cable-net and fabric formwork system, expressive, free-form concrete surfaces can now be constructed efficiently, without the need for complex molds. KnitCandela's thin, double-curved concrete shell with a surface area of almost 538 square feet (fifty square meters) and weighing more than five tonnes, was applied on a KnitCrete formwork of only 121 pounds (fifty-five kilograms). The knitted fabric of the formwork system was carried to Mexico from Switzerland in a suitcase.

 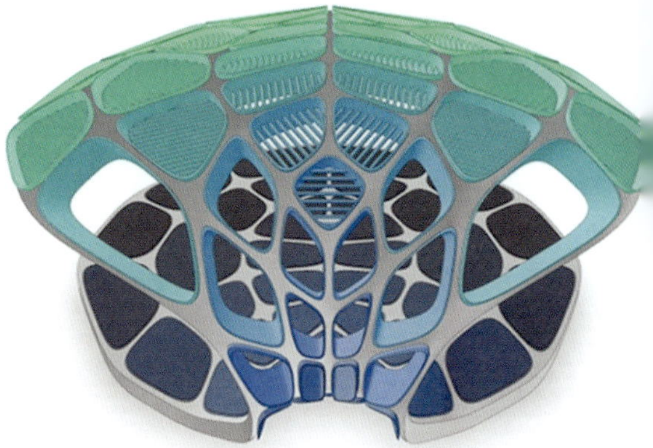

Figs. 86–87: Topology optimization and optimization for fabrication, *VOLU* Dining Pavilion, Zaha Hadid Architects/ZHA CODE, Design Miami 2015

Commissioned by Robbie Antonio for Design Miami 2015, *VOLU* is part of the Revolution Project exploring the application of advanced design and fabrication technologies in the creation of cost-efficient living spaces; as a contemporary dining pavilion that fuses computational design, lightweight engineering, and precision fabrication.

The overall shell form is optimized via particle-spring mesh relaxation. The ribbing pattern was evolved via structural topology optimization. A third optimization process involved material fabrication concerns constraining for straight members and singly curved components (Figs. 86–87).

VOLU's design thus embeds the tectonics of its manufacture within the form itself. Defined by digital processes, the pavilion has been developed with components that are, at most, singly curved and computer programmed to integrate fabrication constraints into the design, while enabling engineering feedback in an iterative delivery process that allows the comprehensive design development of complex and expressive forms through the single curvature bending of flat sheet materials. Comprising a series of structural bands that collect at the spine and expand overhead (Figs. 88–89), the pavilion's patterning is guided by its varied structural loading conditions.

Through analysis of the geometry under load, the pavilion's topology is digitally optimized to remove unnecessary material, resulting in the lightest possible design solution that follows the same organic structural logic found in nature. The pavilion's shape and patterning is guided by structural optimization and fabrication constraints.

Beyond these small-scale experimental explorations done from within our internal research group ZHA CODE, the principles, values, and methods of tectonism have started to inform some of Zaha Hadid Architects' large-scale project realizations. In what follows a small number of these first large-scale results are presented and explained.

Figs. 88–89: *VOLU* Dining Pavilion, Zaha Hadid Architects/ZHA CODE, Design Miami 2015

Figs. 90–91: Aerial view and structural ceiling of the orientation space, Beijing Daxing International Airport, Beijing, China, Zaha Hadid Architects 2018

Beijing Daxing International Airport

Beijing, China, Zaha Hadid Architects 2014–2019

Echoing principles within traditional Chinese architecture that organize interconnected spaces around a central courtyard, the terminal's design guides all passengers seamlessly through the relevant departure, arrival, or transfer zones toward the grand courtyard at its center—a multilayered meeting space at the heart of the terminal.

Five aircraft piers radiate directly from the terminal's main central court where all passenger services and amenities are located, enabling passengers to walk the comparatively short distances through the airport without the need for automated shuttle trains. As a result, the terminal's compact design minimizes distances between check-in and gate, as well as connections between gates for transferring passengers. This radial configuration ensures the farthest boarding gate can be accessed in a walking time of less than eight minutes.

Figs. 92–93: Exterior and interior views of the funnel supports that also function as light wells, Beijing Daxing International Airport, Beijing, China, Zaha Hadid Architects 2018

Structural spans of up to 328 feet (100 meters) create the terminal's generous public spaces and allow the highest degree of flexibility for any future reconfiguration. The roof is composed of six vaulted petals, each lifted up via a major funnel, each of which also brings in natural light.

Natural light also enters the terminal via a network of linear skylights that provides an intuitive system of navigation throughout the building, guiding passengers to and from their departure gates. The roof over the central orientation space is suspended between the six petals and flooded with natural light (Figs. 90–91).

Each of the "petals" is supported by a big funnel that functions like a column with moment connection into the roof surface, but is in fact a development of the roof surface itself (Figs. 92–93). However, this funnel is cut in half and thereby sliced open to function as a light well at the same time.

Beijing Daxing International Airport, Beijing, China,
Zaha Hadid Architects 2014–2019

请勿倚靠，
Please Keep Away

Figs. 94–97: One Thousand Museum, Miami, United States, Zaha Hadid Architects, 2012–2020

One Thousand Museum

Miami, Zaha Hadid Architects 2012–2020

One Thousand Museum is a sixty-two-story residential tower opposite Museum Park in Miami. The tower's design applies and continues Zaha Hadid Architects' research into the use of structural skeletons as the primary ordering and articulation substrate. The differentiated parametric articulation of the tower structure follows the principles of tectonism. The eloquence of parametric articulation stands out against the mute, monotonous seriality of the modernist context.

Figs. 98–100: One Thousand Museum, Miami, United States, Zaha Hadid Architects, 2012–2020

Fig. 101: One Thousand Museum, Miami, United States, Zaha Hadid Architects 2012–2020

The concrete exoskeleton is designed as a web of flowing lines that integrates lateral bracing to withstand Miami's strong wind loads with the members channeling the vertical loads. The accumulation of both vertical and horizontal loads toward the bottom is clearly legible by the way the structure thickens (Figs. 94–97). In the reverse reading the structure becomes lighter toward the top, where the corner columns split to give way for gradually increasing corner windows.

The structural differentiation of the exoskeleton has been utilized for a varied differentiation of apartment types. This differentiation is further accentuated by subtle difference in the articulation of the glazing line in relation to the slabs, generating expansive balconies (Figs. 98–100).

The building incorporates glass-fiber reinforced concrete formwork, which remains in place as construction progresses up the tower. This permanent concrete formwork also was used here for the first time (Fig. 101). It allowed for an accelerated construction and provides the architectural finish that requires minimal maintenance.

One Thousand Museum, Miami, Zaha Hadid Architects 2012–2020

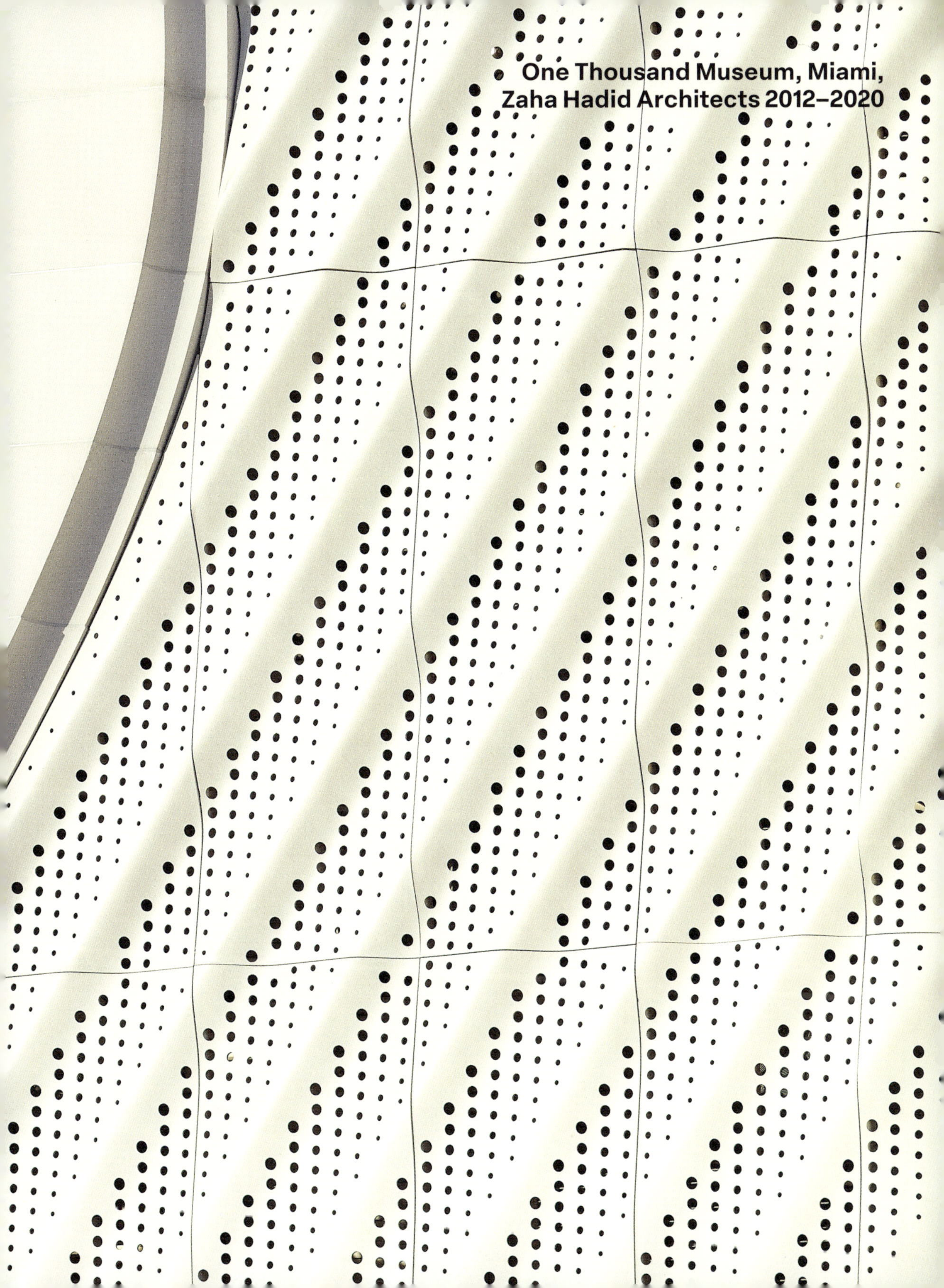

Figs. 102–103: Morpheus Hotel & Resort at City of Dreams, Macau, Chin[a] Zaha Hadid Architect[s] 2013–2018

Morpheus Hotel & Resort at City of Dreams

Macau, China, Zaha Hadid Architects 2013–2018

The underlying diagram of the hotel's design is a pair of towers connected at the ground and roof levels. The central atrium in between these towers runs the height of the hotel and is traversed by external voids that connect the north and south façades (Figs. 102–103).

Three horizontal vortices generate the voids through the building and define the hotel's dramatic internal public spaces. These voids create the urban window that links the hotel's interior communal spaces with the city. In between the free-form voids that traverse the atrium, a series of bridges create unique spaces for the hotel's restaurants, bars, and guest lounges. The atrium's twelve glass elevators provide guests with remarkable views of the hotel's interior and into the city as they travel between the voids of the building.

The atrium void is more than a spectacle. It is a great orientation and navigation space. Taking the elevator is like driving up a vertical street that allows guests to see into all the public spaces they might want to use.

Figs. 104–106: Morpheus Hotel & Resort at City of Dreams, Macau, China, Zaha Hadid Architects 2013–2018

This is the world's most complex high-rise exoskeleton. Its rich pattern of structural members at lower levels progresses upward to a less dense grid of lighter members at its summit (Figs. 104–106). The exoskeleton unburdens the core and allows for dramatic free-flowing interior voids.

Morpheus Hotel & Resort at City of Dreams,
Macau, China, Zaha Hadid Architects 2013–2018

Figs. 107–110: Inkstone House, Cultural Centre by Philip Yuan, Archi-Union Architects, Chengdu, China 2019

Inkstone House, Cultural Centre

Chengdu, Philip Yuan, Archi-Union Architects 2019

While most of the projects selected here to exemplify tectonism are works by Zaha Hadid Architects, this is not meant to imply that Zaha Hadid Architects is alone in pushing tectonism forward. Like parametricism more generally, tectonism is a collective endeavor, an architectural avant-garde movement involving many talents from around the world. In China, Philip Yuan is the movement's most prominent and proliferous protagonists, both with his research and teaching at Tongji University, and with his studio Archi-Union Architects. There are many examples within his oeuvre that could be classified as tectonism. One important aspect in several of his architectural works is the fusion of contemporary computational methodologies with traditional Chinese inspirations and materials. The Inkstone House complex is a good example for Philip Yuan's "parametric regionalism," working with stone and timber and with roof formations that parametrically inflect traditional roof forms (Figs. 107–110).

Philip Yuan's project description reveals how much his work and thinking is aligned with the principles and values of tectonism: "Driven by digital technology, the structural performance-based design, is a process that sets its goal toward seeking the best performance with structural rationality through geometric form-finding calculation, structural performance simulation, and iterative optimization processes. This design approach puts the emphasis on the integration of geometric logic, structural logic, and construction logic, in order to rationally realize the integration of tradition and contemporaneity."

4.3 Environmental Engineering Logics as Drivers of Tectonic Articulation

Tectonism is congenial to the "green" agenda in architecture. The approach is aiming to utilize environmental engineering principles and parameters as formative design inputs. This does not pertain to fuel-efficient machines under the hood—these could be fitted into any building irrespective of its style—but to the principles of a "passive" approach where genuinely architectural parameters, such as global form, orientation, organization, and morphological articulation, come into play. Architectural massing can respond to sun exposure via self-shading, and the envelope articulation can respond via openings and brise-soleil systems. The consideration of wind forces and ventilation flows can be similarly visibly formative. The same applies to drainage or water capture requirements in relation to rainfall. All these features can have a strong impact on the physiognomy of the building. A new level of rigorous parametric shaping of the architecture on the basis of a computationally supported morphological optimization with respect to environmental target parameters can contribute to the emergence of a characterful and memorable visual identity for the project in question. From the gradually differentiated density and direction of shading elements that are distributed across a curved envelope, the orientation of the building can be inferred, also at night and on cloudy days. In this way the building becomes a compass for navigating the surrounding city fabric. This is one more way in which parametric-tectonic design implies the enrichment of the built environment with information, thus contributing to the build-up of information-rich environments that can orient and thus empower users.

The following two projects from Zaha Hadid Architects further illustrate and exemplify how tectonism can work with environmental concerns and make environmental engineering logics formative drivers for both the overall spatial form and for the detailed articulation of a building, and how this enhances urban legibility and navigation.

King Abdullah Petroleum Studies & Research Centre (KAPSARC)

Riyadh, Saudi Arabia, Zaha Hadid Architects 2009–2017

The 7,534,737-square-foot (70,000-square-meter) King Abdullah Petroleum Studies & Research Centre (KAPSARC) campus incorporates five buildings: the Energy Knowledge Centre; the Energy Computer Centre; a Conference Centre with exhibition hall and 300-seat auditorium; a Research Library with archives for 100,000 volumes; and the Musalla, an inspirational place for prayer within the campus. KAPSARC's design has environmental considerations at its heart, drawing the five elements of the campus into a unified whole, around shaded exterior spaces as connective tissue.

Figs. 111–112: King Abdullah Petroleum Studies & Research Centre (KAPSARC), Riyadh, Saudi Arabia, Zaha Hadid Architects 2009–2017

ig. 113: King Abdullah Petroleum Studies & Research Centre (KAPSARC), Riyadh, Saudi Arabia, Zaha Hadid Architects 2009–2017

The primary organizing strategy of the design is a cellular system that integrates different departmental buildings as a single ensemble with interconnecting public spaces. The honeycomb grid is compressed toward its central axis as an extension of the natural wadi that runs to the west (Figs. 111–112).

As Zaha Hadid Architects' first project to be awarded LEED Platinum certification, the center is designed in response to the environmental conditions of the Riyadh Plateau to minimize energy consumption. This has been achieved largely by passive means, i.e., by the organization of the building mass and by the articulation of its envelope. KAPSARC was awarded LEED Platinum certification from the United States Green Building Council (USGBC) through its application of passive and active solutions, including a forty-five percent reduction in energy performance (compared to the ASHRAE baseline standards) achieved via KAPSARC's building massing and orientation, façade optimization, system selection, and the solar PV array located on the roof of the south-facing Conference Centre with a capacity of 5,000 megawatt-hours per year.

The buildings of the campus surround a large public courtyard shaded by canopies supported by a forest of crafted steel columns (Fig. 113). Presenting a solid, protecting shell to the harsh sunlight from the south, the KAPSARC campus opens to north and west; encouraging prevailing winds from the north to cool the courtyard during temperate months and facilitating connections with any future expansion of the campus to the north, as well as creating connections with the researcher's residential community to the west.

King Abdullah Petroleum Studies & Research Centre (KAPSARC),
Riyadh, Saudi Arabia,
Zaha Hadid Architects 2009–2017

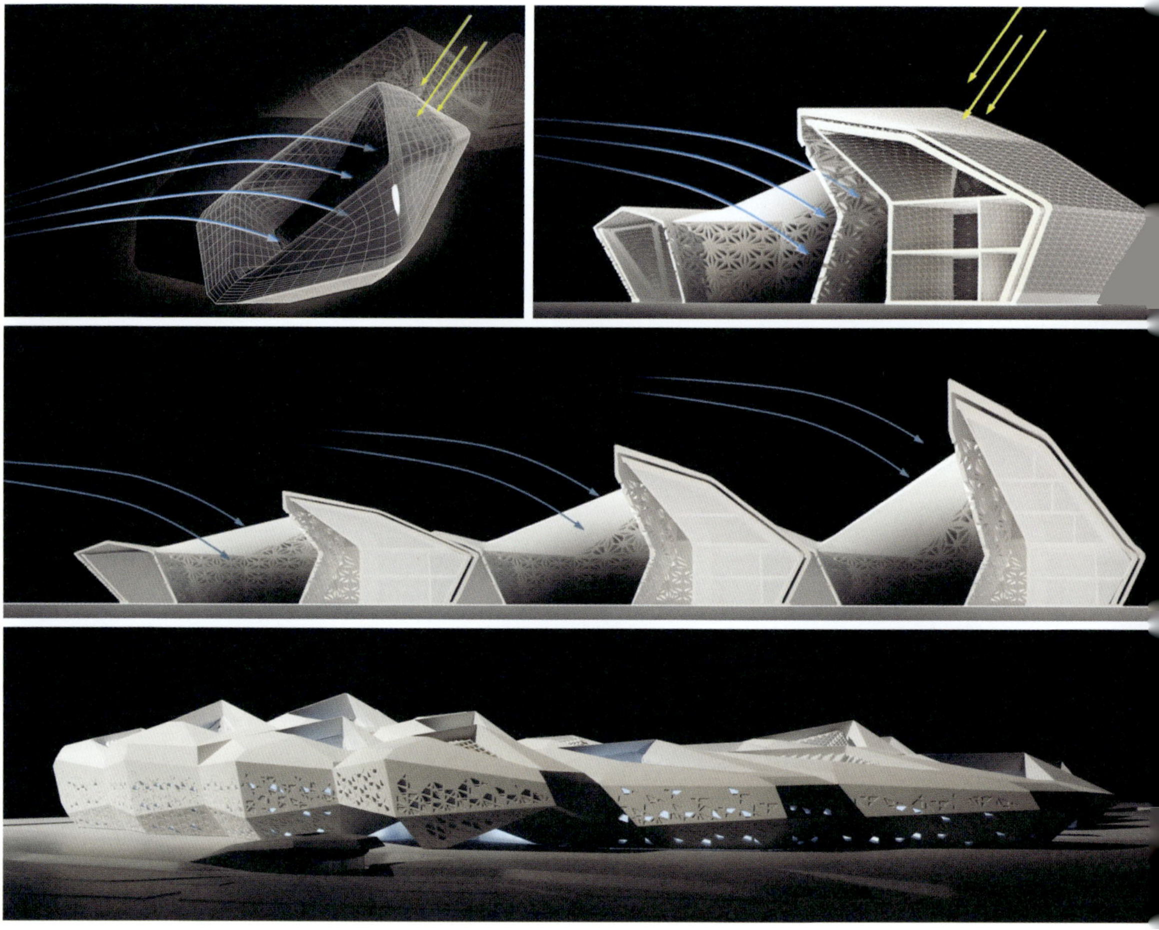

Orientated for the sun and wind conditions, the crystalline forms of the prismatic architectural cells gain in height toward the south, west, and east to shield internal spaces from direct sunlight, while the courtyards within are oriented to the north and northwest to bring indirect sunlight into the spaces below. “Wind catchers” are integrated within the roof profiles on the southern sides of each courtyard to catch the prevailing winds from the north, cooling each courtyard (Figs. 114–117).

Figs. 114–117: King Abdullah Petroleum Studies & Research Centre (KAPSARC), Riyadh, Saudi Arabia, Zaha Hadid Architects 2009–2017

Figs. 118–120: King Abdullah Petroleum Studies & Research Centre (KAPSARC), Riyadh, Saudi Arabia, Zaha Hadid Architects 2009–2017

Two agendas, the agenda of self-shading of open courtyards and glazed atria and the agenda of capturing prevailing winds within the courtyards, harmonize here and can thus collaborate in motivating the tilt of both the solid courtyard forms and the tilt of the shading canopies (Figs. 118–120). The overall sequential stepping up (height increases) in the honeycomb volumes are motivated by the same parameters of wind and sun. The fact that both the building array's roof formation and the formation of the array of canopies are responding in corresponding ways to the sun and wind parameters leads to a morphological similitude between the otherwise very different parts of the building complex. The parametric-tectonic strategy that brings a uniform set of parameters to bear on two otherwise functionally and "ontologically" very different building systems thereby achieves a pleasant formal affiliation of the two systems and thereby enhances the overall expressive unity of the whole building complex. Both systems collaborate in the articulation of an overall field condition that also picks up on and makes visible the underlying wadi as an organizing armature of the larger building complex.

Fig. 121: Central Bank of Iraq, Baghdad, under construction, Zaha Hadid Architects

Central Bank of Iraq

Baghdad, Iraq, Zaha Hadid Architects 2011–2022

Rising from the sloping banks of the Tigris River in Baghdad, the design for the new headquarters of the Central Bank of Iraq conveys the core values at the heart of the institution: solidity, stability, and sustainability.

At a height of 558 feet (170 meters) and a gross internal area of 968,752 square feet (90,000 square meters), the composition of the design is tailored to the very specific constraints of the site. Narrow at its base, the tower widens in the middle to optimize the layout and increase efficiencies, and then tapers inward toward the top (Fig. 121). The grand atrium brings natural light to the heart of the building, opening it to the Tigris River—a constant reference for all bank staff and visitors.

The global form of the tower is highly iconic as its body widens and opens up as it grows upward reminiscent of a plant or flower. This global shape is motivated by the constrained footprint conditions and by the decision to locate the central bank's gold and cash vaults

gs. 122–127: Central ank of Iraq, Baghdad, nder construction, aha Hadid Architects

within the lower part of the tower shaft. These spaces are enclosed in solid concrete. This solid shell then becomes the strong base for an exoskeleton that, according to its structural logic, opens up more and more toward the top, consistent with the inverse cumulation of loads downward. The project is presented here as an example of an environmentally rather than structurally motivated tectonic design because the exoskeleton's form is strongly over-determined by the environmental logic of sun shading. Protection from direct sunlight is indeed an overriding concern and driver for an office building in the hot summer conditions of Baghdad. The fin-shaped columns of the exoskeleton are shaped and oriented so as to minimize the direct sun exposure of the glass façade. This implies that the tower presents a recognizably different look on its north, east, south, and west façades, respectively (Figs. 122–127). While the north façade opens up fully toward the river, the south façade appears completely closed. However, light (but no direct light) is coming in on all sides. The look of the building changes radically as one moves around it due to the organization of the large fixed concrete louvers (that also constitute the primary structure of the building). This effect of observer-dependent differential appearances turns this project into an urban compass.

Central Bank of Iraq, Baghdad, Iraq,
Zaha Hadid Architects 2011–2022

This is important for buildings that function to serve as orienting urban landmarks. Zaha Hadid Architects' Central Bank of Iraq building is such a landmark: it is the only tower in this part of Baghdad.

The iconic character of the building was not the primary goal, but it is certainly a welcome result of the rigorous design process following the methodological principles of tectonism. This kind of memorable and characterful architectural expression that can give identity and orientation to an urban district is typical of the style of tectonism. The fact that these visual-communicative qualities are the result of rational functional reasoning rather than unmediated artistic invention is also typical. This reasoning of tectonism does, however, involve a conscious concern for the appearance and communicative potency of buildings. It thus involves an orchestration and selective-strategic visual heightening of the morphologies that are being derived from the rigorous application of principles of engineering optimization.

4.4. Fabrication Methods as Drivers of Tectonic Articulation

Tectonism delivers both new technical rationalities as well as new articulatory riches that emerge from the new probing attempts to invent and utilize diverse new forms of robotic manufacturing, including various forms of robotic 3D printing. This domain of design drivers is more versatile and open ended than those originating from the computationally enriched engineering logics. Of course, these robotic fabrication drivers are superimposed upon the engineering drivers, imprinting their respective morphological, material, and tectonic characteristics onto a global architectural form that already follows a structural and environmental logic. Every architectural design is co-determined by all these factors—fabrication, structure, environmental parameters—plus, of course, site constraints and urban context, as well as, crucially, the aspects of lay-out organization as an aspect of social functionality. These aspects of site and program are not thematized in this book on tectonism. However, it should be noted as general background understanding that tectonism as a subsidiary style within the framework of the epochal style of parametricism will often deal with rather complex spatial configurations, due to parametricism's principle of adaptive fitting with respect to often irregular site boundaries, and due to the adaptive architectural fitting and differentiation relative to the often complex, nonstandard program mixes and institutional processes that contemporary briefs call for. It is precisely the power of the new, computationally empowered engineering tools and of the new robotic fabrication and construction processes that allows for these complexities to be handled without loss of optimizing rationality and reasonably economical constructability. In the face of this new level of complexity that now enters our discipline, tectonism is uniquely able to maintain a rational spatial order that is experienced as elegance and allows the design to uphold legibility in the face of this functional complexity.

This context of aspirational and achievable complexity must be kept in mind when perusing the rather small-scale and experimental structures that here illustrate and exemplify the agenda of fabrication-driven tectonic articulation.

Arum

Installation for the Venice Architecture Biennale 2012, Zaha Hadid Architects

Arum is a result of research in the design and fabrication of a self-supporting multipanel installation for the Venice Architecture Biennale 2012 and operates against the backdrop of the exciting potentials that the field of curved-crease folding offers in the development of curved surfaces that can be built from aluminum sheets. This self-supporting multipanel shell uses curved-crease folding to generate curved surfaces that can be manufactured from sheet material. The manufacturing process involved the robotic cutting, scoring, and folding of 1/16-inch (1.5-millimeter) aluminum sheets to create the sculpted components that were then bolted together to form the complex double-curved shell that emerged from the patterning without a mold (Figs. 128–130).

The two main challenges were the development of an intuitive design strategy and the production of information adhering to manufacturing constraints. The essential contribution of the research is a proposed form-finding method for curved-crease geometries

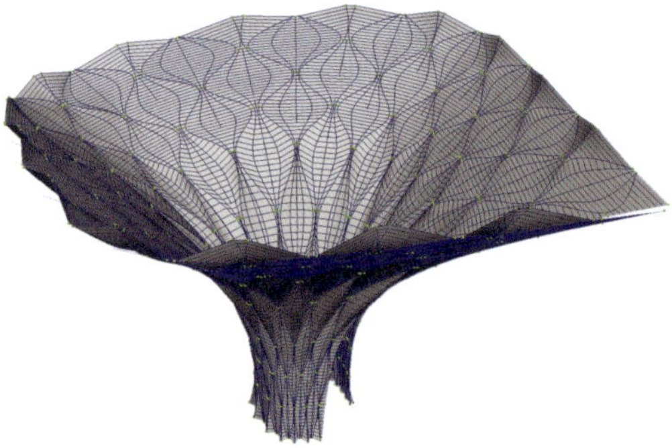

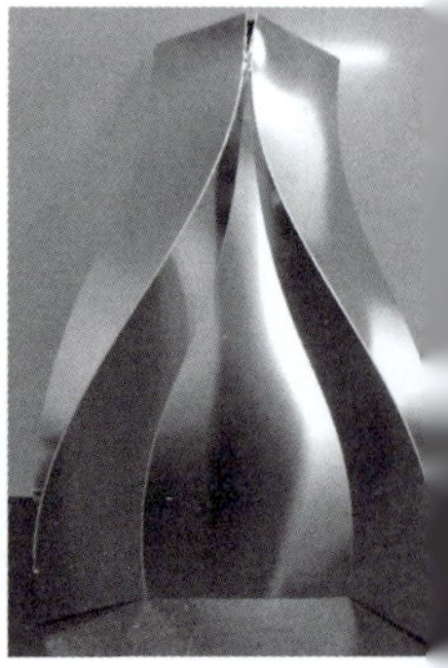

Figs. 128–130: *Arum* manufacturing process, Zaha Hadid Architects/ZHA COD with Buro Happold and RoboFold, Venice Architecture Biennale 2012

that could negotiate the multiple objectives of the ease of use in exploratory design, and the anticipation of manufacturing constraints for architectural-scale assemblies. This much pertains to the aspect of digital tool development that always precedes or accompanies our designs in ZHA CODE. This aspect always relies on tapping into the antecedent work of a scientific research community. The actual design is then simultaneously enabled and constraint by the tool. With *Arum* we aimed at a prototypical, relatively simple design. The crucial idea was to create a something like a hyperboloid over an oval footprint, but, crucially open on one side, so that visitors can enter. The lack of closure also introduced a local weakness in the surface structure that the pleating to some extent was able to compensate for, despite the very thin material.

Figs. 131–133: *Arum* installation, Zaha Hadid Architects/ ZHA CODE, with Buro Happold and RoboFol Venice Architecture Biennale 2012

Once the geometry was designed and optimized it was amenable to robotic fabrication. The aluminum sheets were cut, scored, and folded by means of two collaborating robot arms. The segments were then stacked and shipped to site, where they were bolted together to form the overall surface (Figs. 131–133). The fabrication detail of the bolts adds further character to the overall tectonic articulation.

Vaulted Willow

Public Art Pavilion, Borden Park, Edmonton, Canada, Marc Fornes/ THEVERYMANY 2014

Vaulted Willow is an architectural folly exploring lightweight, self-supporting shells through the development of custom computational protocols of structural form-finding and descriptive geometry. The project's aim is to resolve and delineate structure, skin, and ornamentation into a single unified system. The overall morphology is the result of a reciprocal relationship encompassing experiments in non-linear architectural typology (multiple entries, distributed feet with branching and spiraling legs), structural differentiation (bifurcation of structural download forces, tighter radii of leg profiles for rigidity) and programmatic possibilities for a winding playground (hide and seek).

The surface is formulated through a fabrication strategy of intricate shingles that are assembled into a striated structural skin (Figs. 134–135). The shingles are similar yet unique digitally fabricated stripes that overlap through extended tabs to double material thickness.

The project builds on Marc Fornes's long-term research into self-supporting structures, lightweight monocoque shells made of a series of thin, planar elements proliferating through tangential continuity. The approach uses form-finding protocols to generate structures with extensive double curvature, inherently creating stiffness through geometry and eliminating the need for substructure.

The studies elaborate on the 2D geometry of catenary curves by exploiting a computationally derived dynamic spring network with behavioral attributes. The springs come in various types (tensioners, straighteners), associated with multiple parameters (rest length, angle constraint, strength). The catenary network is first inflated normal to

Figs. 134–135: Vaulted Willow public art pavilion, Borden Park, Edmonton, Canada, Marc Fornes/ THEVERYMANY 2014

the ground plane and as a secondary process inflated outward, normal to the surface to achieve double curvature. The network inflation stagnates as forces equalize, resolving into an optimized structure. Tessellation considerations therefore must be embedded within the topology of the system prior to the inflation process.

Stripes located at the edge of the surface increase tab overlap to help transfer additional loads through lamination and increased connectivity. Porosity increases with height as the structural needs diminish, allowing more light to permeate the space. Running bonds split the stripes, shortening them to ease fabrication, assembly, and decrease material usage through more efficient nesting. Rivet density is also resolved relative to structural needs, with higher densities and varying configurations at bifurcation points, along the edges, and toward the base of the structure. The extensive, computationally driven, descriptive geometry protocol developed for the project embeds axis of bending, angle measurements, part nomenclature, and color information for each stripe.[16]

---

16 Project description/explanation was provided by Marc Fornes.

Zephyr

Pavilion, Texas Tech University, Lubbock, Texas, Marc Fornes/ THEVERYMANY 2019

The Zephyr pavilion offers a shaded passage through the courtyard of the Honors Residence Hall at Texas Tech University in Lubbock, Texas. The pavilion serves as a social anchor at the convergence of countless flows. Duel cantilevers extend from a knot-like center, offering both a signal and a sheltering experience along the campus path (Figs. 136–137). Four densely striped columns expand into bridging arcs, with undulating wings and open-looped columns that define oculi to the sky.

Figs. 136–137: Zephyr pavilion, Texas Tech University, Lubbock, Texas, United States, Marc Fornes/ THEVERYMANY 2019

Science Museum Benches

Robotic hot-wire cutting, ZHA CODE, London 2014–2016

Through the development of concrete benches for the Science Museum's Mathematics Gallery in London, the design constraints of robotic hot-wire cutting of EPS formwork is being piloted for high-performance concrete structures.

The robotic hot-wire cutting of polystyrene molds is about thirty times faster than that of CNC milling. Like all numerically controlled fabrication processes, the unique customization of each mold and thus each cast object is possible. To be sure, hot-wire cutting imposes its own geometric constraints onto every one of its products, namely all surfaces are either flat or ruled surfaces. Ruled surfaces are surfaces where for every point on the surface there is at least one straight line on the surface through the point. The hot wire is stretched into a straight line and then freely swept through space. The curvature of the resulting surface is mostly anticlastic (although flat, cylindrical, and conic surfaces are also possible subsets). To produce a closed volume from such surfaces requires the introduction of curved creases or edges where these surfaces meet. These geometric constraints are shared by all (otherwise infinite) variants and are the price for the rapid and efficient cutting process. The fact that the resulting forms all share this characteristic and easily recognizable morphology is, for the purposes of expressive, semiological articulation, a feature rather than a bug. In our Mathematics Gallery we were thereby able to distinguish and bring together two distinct, yet related, families of forms: the forms based on ruled surfaces (Figs. 138–139) and the forms based on minimal surfaces (Fig. 56). These types of surfaces are recognizably distinct as well as recognizably similar, thus allowing us to articulate unity across differences. The materiality played along with this pursuit: smooth light-gray concrete surfaces complement off-white stretched fabric surfaces.

Figs. 138–139: Science Museum Benches, robotic hot-wire cutting, ZHA CODE, London, United Kingdom 2014–2016

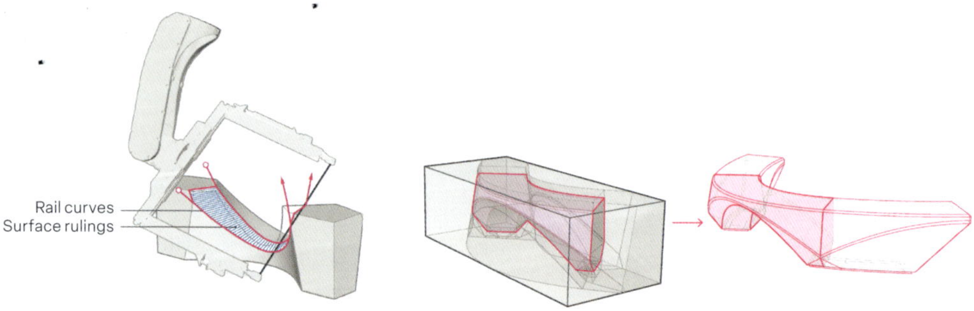

igs. 140–142: *Thallus*, ʼinacoteca di Brera, ⁄ilan Design Week, aha Hadid Architects .017

Thallus

Pinacoteca di Brera, Milan Design Week, Zaha Hadid Architects 2017

Created by automated additive manufacturing as well as hot-wire cutting technology, the *Thallus* structure (Figs. 140–142) presents the ongoing investigations into robotic assisted design undertaken by the ZHA CODE research group; demonstrating what can now be achieved in terms of mechanization and customization in the architecture, construction, and engineering industries. Six-axis robotic 3D printing technology created the four-mile (seven-kilometer) extruded structural strip as a continuous line that repeatedly loops to connect with itself on a ruled surface. Ruled surfaces created via hot-wire cutting have been applied in the fabrication process of the formwork onto which the continuous structural strip has been robotically 3D printed.

For the robotic printing toolpath, the design explores differential growth methods through expansion and diffusion arising from a single continuous seed curve guided iteratively via simulation parameters while constrained to a reference surface. Density gradation and direction of growth have been defined by parameters such as proximity to boundaries, angled direction of rulings as well as structural requirements. The result is a porous filigree shell. The material extrusion pattern integrates morphogenetic process parameters with structural and fabrication rationalities as determinants of an intriguing intricacy that is reminiscent of the beauty of organic nature.

ACADIA 3D Printed Chair

Zaha Hadid Architects (ZHA CODE), presented at ACADIA 2014

The design exploits the nearly limitless geometric complexity and fineness of manufacture afforded by high-resolution 3D-printing technologies. The printed chair design emerged from several successive optimization processes: After the outer edge line was modeled, the surface was generated via mesh relaxation with Kangaroo. This surface was then the input for a structural topology optimization to generate a pattern of reinforcement lines via iterative subtraction. The pattern was then interpreted via two gradient geometric manipulations: first by thinning/thickening the surface depth, and secondly by increasing the perforation between the lines of the emergent ribbing network (Figs. 143–145).

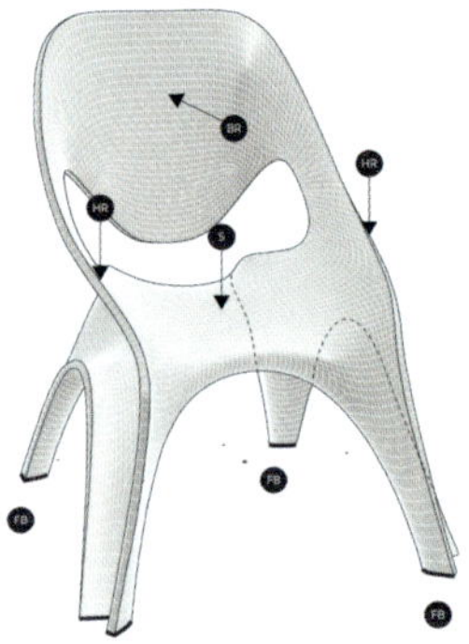

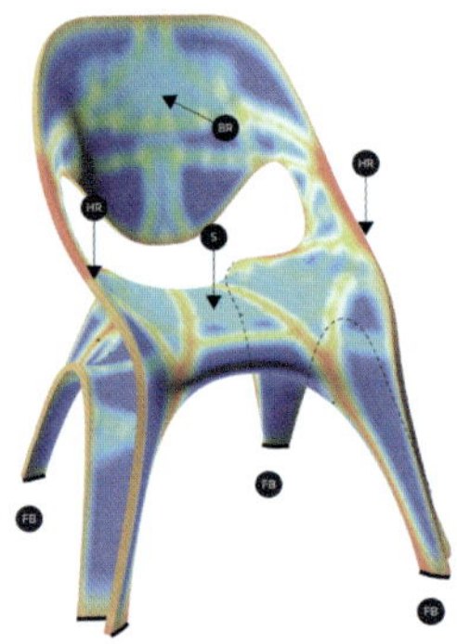

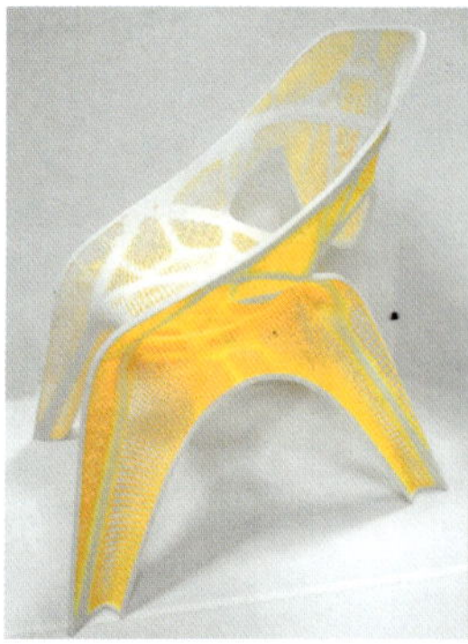

Figs. 143–145: *ACADIA 3D Printed Chair*, Zaha Hadid Architects (ZHA CODE), printed by Stratasys, presented at ACADIA 2014

Topology optimization, a field of structural mechanics, has found increased application in architectural design in recent times. Topology optimization is a generative design process that delivers an intricately differentiated pattern of optimal material channeling of loads or forces. As architects we value the resultant organic beauty. The characterful articulation becomes both an ornament and semiological communication medium when orchestrated within an overarching architectural system of signification, e.g., for a complex corporate interior landscape. Within this architectural design agenda, quick qualitative results that provide interactive feedback to the designer are just as important as the accurate, material-saving results. This design-research and the prototype investigate the potentials of using topology optimization in the context of design—where the results are visible as opposed to the usual utilitarian case when the results are not visibly expressed. Additionally, it attempts to incorporate the novel opportunities of manufacture afforded by high-resolution 3D-printing technologies.

The research attempts the integration of topology optimization into an early design pipeline and highlights the difficulties thereof. It faces similar challenges of computational time as other Finite Element Method–based simulations. Machine learning techniques have been previously applied to alleviate similar problems in Computational Fluid Dynamics. This research investigates the use of learning algorithms to improve the computation times of topology optimization. Specifically, it focuses on the use of such techniques for topology optimization of thin-shell, minimal surface geometries and the incorporation of specific assumptions related to such geometries to improve the accuracy of the statistical approximation.[17]

Nagami Chairs: Rise, Bow

3D robotic printing by Nagami, Zaha Hadid Architects 2018

The Nagami chairs (Figs. 146–151) have been printed with a pellet-extruder employing raw plastic particles rather than a filament. The chosen plastic is PLA, a non-toxic, biodegradable material from renewable sources such as cornstarch, which ensures sustainability, plus lightness and stability.

17 Project description/explanation was contributed by ZHA CODE.

Figs. 146–147: Nagami Chairs: Rise (left), Bow (right); 3D robotic printing by Nagami, Zaha Hadid Architects 2018

Figs. 148–151: Nagami Chair: Bow; 3D robotic printing by Nagami, Zaha Hadid Architects 2018

The chairs combine pristine design informed by structural optimization processes typically found in nature with innovative materials and advanced additive fabrication methods. The pattern and material gradient concur in articulating the load path or flow of forces through the object under life load.

Striatus Bridge

Venice Architecture Biennale 2021, Zaha Hadid Architects with Block Research Group

Exhibited at the Giardini della Marinaressa during the Venice Architecture Biennale until November 2021, the fifty-two-by-thirty-nine-foot (sixteen-by-twelve-meter) footbridge is the first of its kind, combining traditional techniques of master builders with advanced computational design, engineering, and robotic manufacturing technologies. The 3D printing process can be used to build load-bearing concrete structures that require significantly less material and no steel reinforcement or mortar. Striatus is an arched, unreinforced masonry footbridge composed of 3D-printed concrete blocks assembled without mortar. The name "Striatus" reflects its structural logic and fabrication process. Concrete is printed in layers orthogonal

Figs. 152–155: Striatus Bridge, Venice Architecture Biennale 2021, Zaha Hadid Architects with Block Research Group

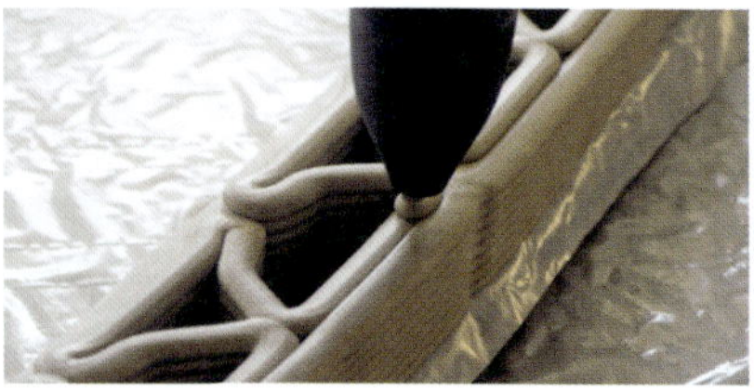

Figs. 156–158:
Striatus Bridge, Venice Architecture Biennale 2021, Zaha Hadid Architects with Block Research Group

to the main structural forces to create a "striated" compression-only funicular structure that requires no reinforcement (Figs. 152–158).[18]

Tectonism is a new paradigm and style in architecture and design. Much of its production is still small-scale academic experiments, or "artworks" displayed in exhibitions. New aesthetic sensibilities are here as much tested as are technological feasibilities, rendering a possible future viscerally tangible, and querying its desirability with test audiences. These works query technological, aesthetic, and anthropological innovations. Fabrication technology experimentation becomes here an engine of spatio-formal invention that in turn might inspire potential socio-programmatic invention.

---

18 Project description/explanation was contributed by ZHA CODE.

Striatus Bridge, Venice Architecture Biennale 2021, Zaha Hadid Architects with Block Research Group

Fig. 159: *Puddle Chair*, Zaha Hadid Design with AI Build, presented at "Meta-Utopia—Between Process and Poetry," ZHD Gallery, London 2017. This chair was designed specifically to be manufactured v free-form, multicolor (black and blue) robotic 3D printing. The sofa's space frame is optimized fo lightness, material robustness, and structural integrity, and its intricate design is layered with an artificial cloth to transform it into a comfortable seating surface with a stimulating ripple surface texture.

Fig. 160: *Cirratus*, 3D-printed concrete vase, ZHA CODE, fabrication by XtreeE London/Paris 2017. The design is an interpretation of a classic vase by architect Alvar Aalto. A bespoke algorithm produces complex double curvature geometry that adher to and exploits the specific concrete printing manufacturi constraints and expresses the additiv layer-by-layer proces of its making.

In a 2017 exhibition entitled "Meta-Utopia—Between Process and Poetry" hosted by the Zaha Hadid Design Gallery in London, we displayed a diverse range of current experiments in robotic fabrication, including large-scale multimaterial 3D printing, robotic plastic extrusion capable of printing lines into space without molds, concrete printing, robotic component assembly, robotic hot-wire cutting, as well as robotic curved folding of sheet materials (Figs. 159, 160). Each of these fabrication techniques imprints its unique, unmistakable character onto its products, including the shape-range of the overall form as well as the materiality and texture. This means that the concept of *faktura* is well alive in our era of robotics.[19] This new diversity of form-making potentials and aesthetic expressions affords a welcome expansion of parametricism's repertoire beyond the smooth nurb surfaces that had been prevalent previously. This fuels both programmatic invention as well as semiological articulation. According to my theory of architectural autopoiesis, new styles manifest both new formal concepts as well as a new conception of program or social function, each connected with the opportunities afforded by new technologies. The proliferating diversity of social interaction patterns is inherently hungry for new expressive formal identities. Tectonism can deliver the demanded richness, while maintaining a consistent twenty-first-century feel, thereby able to avoid falling back on retro styles. The originality of a unique twenty-first-century expression is guaranteed by the fact the underlying shaping technologies have only become available in the twenty-first century.

---

19 *Faktura* is the visual trace of the fabrication process in the artifact or work of art. It is seen as a positive character-sponsoring quality of the artifact or artwork. The concept emerged in the context of the Russian avant-garde art and design during the early Soviet Union era.

Parametric Dinner Jacket

Patrik Schumacher with Vasilija Zivanic, London/New York 2013

This jacket is my first foray into fashion design. Mainstream fashion design has not yet woken up to the design potentials of the computational age, nor to the ethos of technologically sophisticated performance-driven design. While I have no intention to focus on fashion, it was important to me to contribute to innovation in fashion. My attitude here, i.e., the attitude of tectonism, is not primarily functionalist with respect to the practical functioning of clothes. However, an up-to-date practical functioning on the basis of contemporary technology and contemporary lifestyle requirements are a necessary base condition for any twenty-first century fashion articulation. On top of this base a rich versatile expressive differentiation of outfits, with respect to the semiological articulation of complex identities relative to a diversity of situational occasions, become possible, thereby delivering toward the social communicative functionality of fashion design. Clues toward contemporary technological base requirements can be taken from contemporary sportswear as well as underwear engineering and fabrication. Non-ironing and quick drying are just the most basic requirements. On top we can have movement management via differential stiffness and elasticity, as well as temperature management and moisture management, calling for differential thickness, absorption capacity, perforation, and so forth. For all these functional sophistications the technology of computationally differentiated fabric qualities can offer solutions, either via tailoring and assembling different but related fabrics or via weaving or knitting a gradient of continuously transforming fabrics. The articulation of hybrid identities and even the transformation from one expression into another, i.e., from a sportive casual occasion into a more formal-representative occasion, the switch from a cycling or jogging exercise into a business meeting, should become possible. These are ideas that could only be translated into reality by a technologically sophisticated manufacturer or brand. My initial experimentation with tectonism in fashion is only hinting at this new untested potential.

Figs. 161–162: *Parametric Dinner Jacket*, Patrik Schumacher with Vasilija Zivanic, London/New York 201

The *Parametric Dinner Jacket* (Figs. 161–162) is made from neoprene fabric, which is super light, warm, and elastic. The elasticity allows the tailoring to follow the body shape closely without compromising movement and comfort. Zippers substitute for buttons everywhere. Laser-cut perforation patterns allow for ventilation where needed and also enhance elasticity, as well as delivering an additional substrate for ornamental/semiological expression. The idea is to offer an elegant formal evening jacket perfect to go jogging in right after the event.

4.5. From Semiological Form-to-Function Correlations to a Systematic Visual-Spatial Language

Architecture is here theorized with respect to its contribution to societal progress, namely its performance regarding the innovative spatial ordering of increasingly complex cooperative social processes. As social processes become more diverse, complex and intricate control must increasingly rely of self-control of increasingly free and self-directed actors. Accordingly, the architectural ordering must increasingly shift its mode of operation from the use of controlling physical barriers to the use-communicated thresholds. Architecture's social performativity thus depends on the information-richness and communicative capacity of its products. This posits the task of designing the built environment as a system of signification employing a designed visual-spatial language. Architectural semiology becomes the key to the upgrading of the discipline's social performance.

The movement of tectonism is well placed to consciously take up this societal task of architecture. However, this has not yet happened, despite making this argument and urging to focus on this task in my essay in AD's *Parametricism 2.0: Rethinking Architecture's Agenda for the 21st Century*. The current book is another attempt to steer the movement toward this enlarged level of ambition, which would require a further collective wave of design research.

Much of the current design experimentations are exploring new technologies. Architects are thus inevitably drawn into engineering problematics and become proto-engineers, stirring and steering real engineers to come on board. However, it is important to keep track of the fundamental difference between the design disciplines (including architecture) on the one hand and the engineering disciplines on the other hand. The demarcation between design and engineering is based on the distinction of the social functioning of the built environment from its technical functioning. The clear demarcation of competencies is all the more important the closer the collaboration must become with respect to the complex ambitions we pursue in our built environments. While the technical functioning considers the physical integrity, constructability, and physical performance of the building, architecture and design must take into consideration that a building's social function, i.e., its function to order social processes, succeeds via visual legibility. The core competency of architecture/design is thus the task of articulation. However, according to the style and thesis of tectonism, it is the new engineering and fabrication logics that deliver the expressive repertoire of articulation to architecture and design. This double burdening of form selection—where technical and communicative performance must be considered simultaneously—becomes possible only due to the expansive proliferation of technically viable options, so that an additional selection criterion that selects and composes an orchestrated subset of all technically feasible forms, according to compositional/legibility concerns, also becomes possible.

Ideally, the expressive repertoire of tectonism is used to build up project-specific systems of signification. The idea I would like to put forward here is that an enhanced communicative articulation should not be a constraint to work with a lexicon of visual icons that express various designated social situations in a one-to-one mapping. Instead, our ambition with respect to the semiological project is to create a visual-spatial language that utilizes the combinatorial power of grammar to enhance its expressive potency.

Until now, there is no built example of a project that has been conceived like this. However, I have, over the years, guided several academic design research projects to explore this possibility via speculative design projects with student groups, most prominently at the Design Research Laboratory at the Architectural Association School of Architecture in London.

The task was to design a project-specific visual-spatial semiological system. For these academic design research studies, we chose programs such as a university campus or a corporate campus for tech firms like Google, and innovative work environments in general, as the initial design research arena for the semiological project. These are the high-performance arenas at the most advanced frontier of our civilization where the new productivity potentials of our post-Fordist epoch are explored and pushed forward. Architecture's innovations must be relevant and congenial to these arenas. It is here that the complexity of social processes is most expressed, where communication is most intense and dynamic, where diverse human actions and interactions are integrated in intricate patterns of cooperation rather than just run in parallel. In contrast, retail or residential arenas are much simpler, and less integrated, i.e., they accommodate parallel rather than integrated lives and thus, as it were, operate by addition rather than multiplication. The next decision was to privilege interior over exterior spaces. While urban fabrics matter, it is in the interior where the most important and most intricate social interactions reside.

As an example of a semiologically conceived architectural project, this chapter presents a recent student project developed by Yihui Wu, Lei Wang, and Yanling Xu under the guidance of myself and Pierandrea Angius at the Design Research Laboratory of the Architectural Association School of Architecture in London. The semiological design research project crucially includes the design of a visual-spatial language, i.e., the design of a semiological system or system of signification, with explicit vocabulary and grammar. The design project is then understood as only one among many possible applications or "utterances" of the designed language.

All semiological design must proceed by means of building up two correlated systems of distinctions, the system of signifiers or symbols, and the system of signifieds or meanings. This focus on system and distinction is crucial and was first emphasized by the founder of semiology, the Swiss linguist Ferdinand de Saussure. All terms are relative and acquire their meaning only in distinction and relation to the other terms. A language operates always on the basis of a total system of distinctions "in which all the elements fit together, and in which the value of any one element depends on the simultaneous coexistence of all the others."[20] In the design of a semiological system the distinctions in the domain of the signifiers are to be correlated with the distinctions in the meaning domain. In the case of architectural semiology, the domain of the signifier is the world of architectural forms, i.e., the spaces and their defining components or properties, and the domain of the signified is the world of varied possible social situations to be accommodated.

The project presented here proposes a work environment for a start-up incubator. In such buildings many different social situations must be distinguished and therefore many different spaces must be differentially characterized. Each space within the total manifold of spaces is defined by a particular combination of aspects. The design of each individual space therefore involves several appropriate selections from the articulation options made available by the language via its vocabulary and grammar. The vocabulary is ordered into categories, or substitution classes, or registers of semiological encoding: location, spatial shape, boundary type, color, or material, for instance. These registers correspond to meaning dimensions within which the intended aspects of the social situation can thus be selected: destination versus circulation, business versus socializing, work versus meet, public versus private, allocated versus bookable, and so forth.

---

20 Ferdinand de Saussure, *Course in General Linguistics* (French: *Cours de linguistique générale*), Geneva 1916: p. 113.

The first distinction we might introduce to explain the designed system is the formal distinction between bound versus unbound spaces. The bound/unbound spatial distinction (on the signifier side) corresponds to social meaning, i.e., the distinction between business spaces and leisure spaces. This formal distinction carries the further functional meaning of destination versus circulation space. Within the bounded business spaces, we introduce the subsidiary distinction of convex versus concave spaces, designed to encode the social distinction between workspaces and meeting spaces. In the unbound leisure spaces this distinction between concave versus convex is also meaningful by signifying collective (meeting) versus individually used spaces.

The posited distinctions, both the distinction bound/unbound as well as distinction convex/concave, are rather abstract and therefore allow for a lot of variation in shape and size without thereby infringing on the distinctive meanings preserved across all the possible variations. This is indicated in the small diagrams at the bottom (Fig. 163). This abstractness allows for parametric variation, in line with the requirements of parametricism. We might therefore talk about "parametric semiology."

Fig. 163: Dictionary of visual-spatial vocabulary: Two hierarchically ordered distinctions in the register of spatial shape—the spatial distinction bound versus unbound signifies the social distinction business versus leisure. Within the bound spaces the spatial distinction convex versus concav signifies the social distinction meeting versus working.

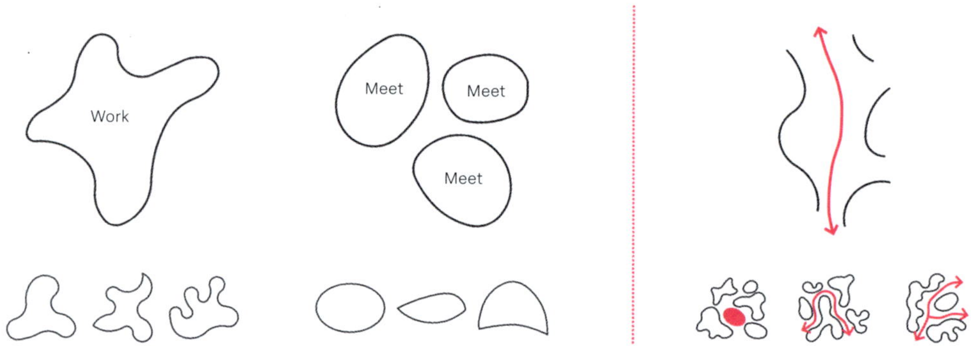

Now we introduce two further distinctions that both cut across the previously introduced distinctions as well as cut across each other. Both meeting and workspaces might be private, semiprivate, or public, respectively represented via thick boundary, dashed boundary, or thin boundary. Public work/meet areas might be WeWork–style coworking areas. Private areas belong to particular start-up companies. Color, i.e., gray versus white, further encodes allocated versus bookable spaces. The matrix indicates that the choices offered by these distinctions are freely combinable. Of course, it must be

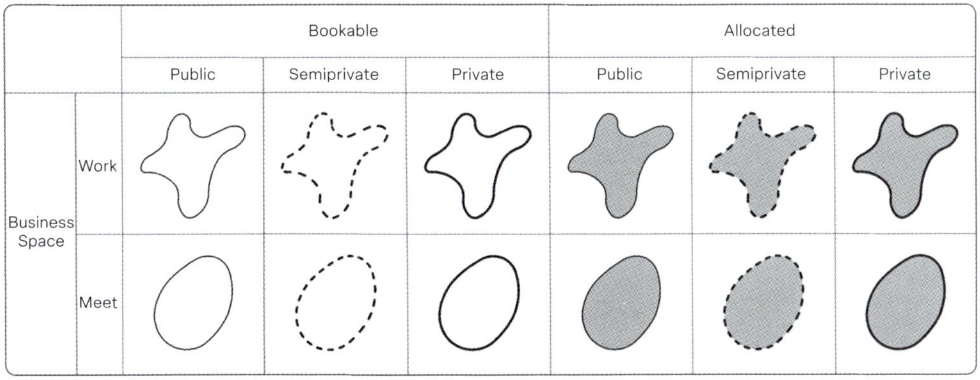

Fig. 164: This matrix shows how three distinctions can combine to produce twelve different expressions.

checked if all possible combinations make sense on the meaning side. If not, then restrictions on free combination(s) must be introduced. Such restrictions or their absence, i.e., the regulation of sign-radical combinations, are determined in the grammar of the language.

We can see here how grammar-based languages operate by multiplication, by exploiting the proliferation of expressive power due to the power of combinatorics. The system of three distinctions offers here the expression of twelve different messages (Fig. 164). If we would include the bound/unbound distinction in this game of combination we would arrive at twenty-four expressions.

Another aspect of the paradigm of parametric semiology is the readiness to consider that distinctions might be introduced not as strict dichotomies but as a gradient spectrum of options defined

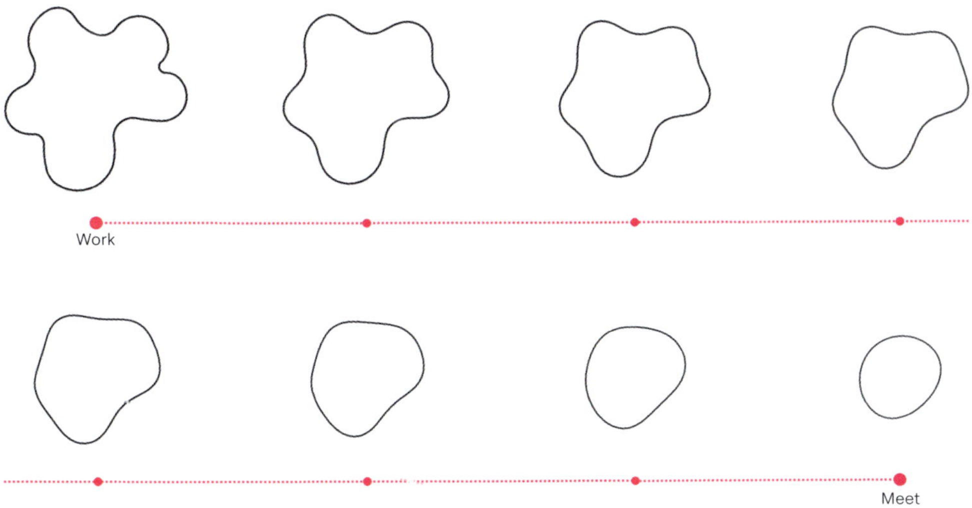

Fig. 165: Parametric semiology: The dichotomy of convex versus concave is transformed into a continuous spectrum of shapes defined between the two poles with a continuum of shapes that are more or less convex or concave.

by two poles. Formally this can be achieved by "in-betweening" or "morphing" between the two poles of the spectrum (Fig. 165). However, this operation only makes sense if we can meaningfully conceive of a corresponding gradient in the domain of social meaning. Within contemporary work dynamics such a spectrum of situations between a clear-cut meeting situation on the one hand and a clear-cut concentrated individual work situation on the other hand could indeed make sense. If we assume a gradation into eight grades and combine these eight choices with the two new distinctions introduced above we arrive at ninety-six choices offered by working with only three distinctions.

As indicated above, the grammar of a language regulates the combination of sign-radicals into full signs as well as regulating the combination of multiple signs into a larger communication or overall text. It is therefore required to design and thus decide on the syntactic rules for combining signs and related semantic rules about how the combination of sign-radicals or signs should be read to determine the overall meaning of the combined signs. It can be expected that the downstream combination of the designed vocabulary might create problems and is thus constraining and feeding back into the design of the vocabulary. The diagrams here test the possibility of combining work and meeting spaces and show that the convex meeting spaces can and should nestle into the concave niches provided by the working spaces. Further adjacent workspaces are expected to similarly interlock. We can thus posit the grammatical rule of nesting spaces (Fig. 166).

Fig. 166: Grammar of nesting spaces: The vocabulary of concave and convex spaces lends itself to the organization of efficient aggregations. Nesting also indicates that spaces belong together.

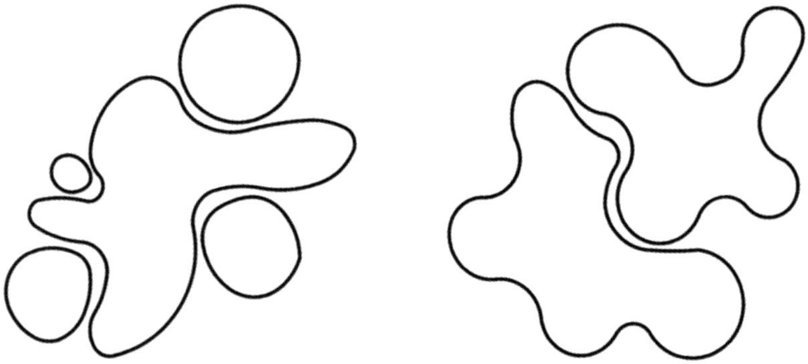

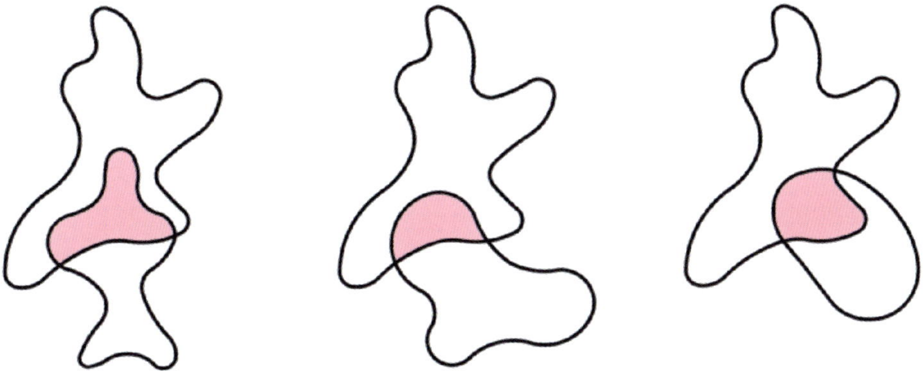

Fig. 167: Grammar of overlap conditions: Two concave work zones generate a new concave workspace that belongs to both. Alternatively, they might generate and overlap in a shared convex meeting space. A work zone and a meeting zone can generate a new meeting space. These results make sense and are coherent with the initial definitions.

Within contemporary architecture, since deconstructivism, it is possible and often advantageous to allow for territories to overlap. As social complexity and communicative intensity increases it becomes increasingly problematic to restrict the spatial organization of social processes to neatly separated zones. Rather than jumping from this order of zoning to a disordered condition where everything mixes everywhere, it is advantageous to allow for the determinate allocation and articulation of zones where particular social functions and their respective territories can overlap. The accommodation of this possibility is a recurring feature of parametric semiology. There is no guarantee that any given vocabulary can support the meaningful and coherent articulation of overlap conditions. The vocabulary introduced here does allow for the articulation of overlap, while maintaining a coherent system of signification. The overlap of two concave, amoeba-like workspaces might generate either a new concave workspace, i.e., where two work groups might collaborate in a dedicated collaboration zone, or might generate a new convex space as shared meeting space that then conspicuously belongs to both workspaces that overlap there. The overlap between a concave work zone and a convex meeting zone generates a new convex meeting space. This can make sense when a meeting space that belongs to a particular work group is at the same time characterized as belonging to a larger meeting zone (Fig. 167). Two overlapping convex meeting zones would generate a new convex meeting zone, belonging to both.

The next move is building up the complexity of the semiological system that tackles the initial distinction between bound and unbound spaces. This distinction is a dichotomy with a clear-cut criterion: a bounded space is enclosed by a boundary. The unbounded space is the continuous space that flows between these bounded spaces. This criterion still holds in case of a long, meandering boundary line, if it eventually closes the loop. However, this distinction can be made ambiguous, and turned into an ordered spectrum, distinguishing degrees of boundedness. On the one side of the spectrum the distinction is clear and crisp as bounded spaces are indeed always fully closed. However, spaces might be defined that are very similar to fully bounded spaces where the boundary loop nearly closes but leaves a small gap. These gaps might gradually increase and the distinction between bounded and unbound spaces becomes increasingly blurred. On the meaning side this can be interpreted as follows: the distinction between business spaces for formal collaboration and spaces for socializing is getting blurred. A field that offers many such in-between situations might be desirable and conducive to informal communication and collaboration.

Fig. 168: Gradient field condition: The dichotomy of bound versus unbound spaces is gradually dissolved moving from west (left) to east (right). The distinction between work and meet is being maintained as the distinction between business and socializing communication is being increasingly blurred.

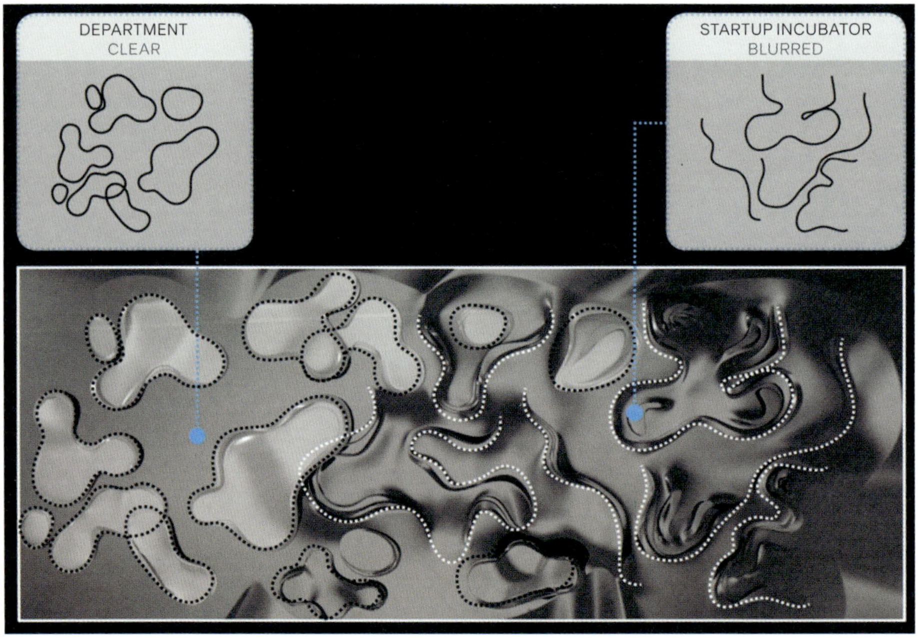

The project utilizes this possibility offered by the semiological system. In particular, it does so by arranging the spaces in such a way that an east-to-west vector of gradual transformation emerges whereby the distinction between bound and unbound spaces that is very crisp at the western end of the space gradually dissolves as we move eastwards (Fig. 168). This implies that the morphological encoding of the difference between formal/informal business is redundantly over-coded by the locational encoding. Such redundancies are a useful option in cases where messages deserve to be reinforced because they might otherwise be overlooked or where messages are important and thus deserve emphasis via duplication. The model displays a further redundancy: the gradient from the zone with the crisp bound/unbound dichotomy to the blurred condition is once more reinforced by a gradient treatment of the contrastive color distinction, which gradually disappears as we move into the blurred condition (Fig. 169). In turn, the ordered gradient spectrum also offers locational information and thus also operates as an effective navigation aid.

In the further detailing of the three-dimensional articulation of the scheme the boundary lines themselves blur and turn from platform edges and walls more and more into relief-like stepping edges as we move into the blurred zone and as the closure of these lines diminishes. Thus, users gain multiple local morphological clues that tell them where in the spectrum from formal to informal they are located. As the detailed model shows (Figs. 170–171), the distinction between working and meeting zones can also, to some extent, be maintained in the informal, blurred zones.

Fig. 169: The field three-dimensionally articulated and rnished. The bound–unbound west–east adient is redundantly over-coded via the gradual dissolution of the light–dark color contrast.

gs. 170–171: Detailed three-dimensional articulation of the blurred end of the gradient spectrum. The boundary itself is dissolving while the distinction between working and meeting holds fast.

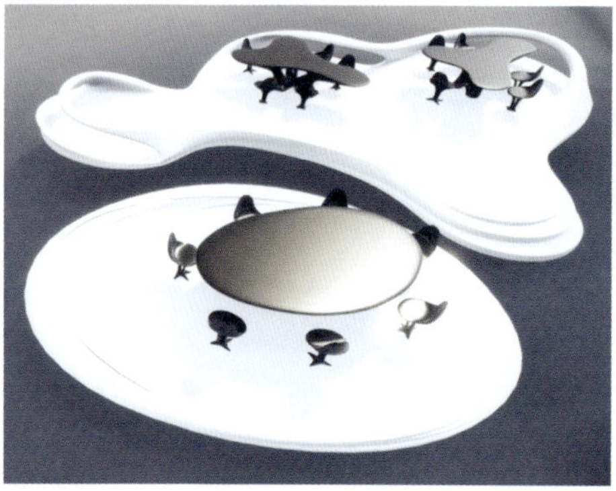

Finally, the semiological system also encompasses and makes semiological use of the furniture as well as of the ceiling and lighting design. The design succeeds in reusing the correlation of the convex/concave distinction with the meet/work distinction on the furniture scale (Figs. 172–173). The ability to reuse distinctions in this way is of course elegant and advantageous and makes the overall language cognitively less taxing. Also, the choice of forms has been motivated here by considerations of pragmatic social functionality. Convex tables and convex spaces make sense as meeting tables and spaces. Its opposite, the concave or convoluted, meandering form is viable for both work tables and work zones (Figs. 174, 175).

Figs. 172–173: The distinction of meet/work via the differenc convex/concave is being re-applied on the level and scale of the furniture.

Fig. 174: The crisp, formal, dichotomous end of the space in first-person perspective.

Fig. 175: The blurred, informal end of the space in first-person eye-level perspective.

This example shows that while signifiers, with respect to their communication function, can in principle be chosen arbitrarily, this is not always possible or advisable in architectural semiology. Here the domain of the signifier is indeed often preconstrained to the range of forms that are pragmatically viable for the purposes they are to signify. What we further witness here is that the relative arbitrariness or degrees of freedom that exist at the outset when starting to design a semiological system become increasingly constrained by what has already been stipulated. We should expect that architectural codes, just like verbal languages, expand their vocabulary by analogical extension rather than by arbitrary invention.

This example is meant to illustrate how a relatively complex and nuanced semiological project can be step-wise developed on the basis of an integrated, systematic series of simple and intuitive form-function or form-meaning correlations. It serves here as an initial illustrative glimpse into the ambitious project of a generalized architectural semiology.

This design research program serves to upgrade the discipline's capacity to enhance the social performance of the built environment by increasing its information density and communicative power.

This AADRL project is a successful design research effort in parametric semiology. It uses the stylistic repertoires of foldism, blobism, and swarmism, but not yet the rigors and expressive powers of tectonism. It is easy to imagine how the repertoires of these earlier forms of parametricism could have been substituted by the repertoires of tectonism. However, it is easier to imagine this than to do it in a competent way that also satisfies the underlying engineering rationalities. For the AADRL students it would have required another complete learning cycle to acquire these sophisticated competencies.

Following, as an illustration of the possibility of the utilization of characteristic tectonic features that originate from engineering logics, four experimental academic structures (pavilions) have been selected and arranged into a matrix that suggests a potential semiological utilization. These are four of the research pavilions annually constructed on the campus of the architecture faculty of Stuttgart University. These pavilions are sophisticated and highly original exemplars of tectonism. They are the creation of student teams working under the guidance of professors Achim Menges and Jan Knippers. Achim Menges represents architecture with his Institute of Computational Design and Construction (ICD) and Jan Knippers represents engineering with his Institute of Building Structures and Structural Design (ITKE). To be sure, these pavilions have not been conceived in connection with the idea of semiology. Nor were they conceived together as an integral system of buildings or building morphologies that could be related in a systematic semiological way as connected parts of a larger complex of spaces. However, this does not prevent us here from selecting and relating these independently conceived morphologies and to imagine them to be part of a system of signification. While all four pavilions are unique, there are both strong similarities and conspicuous differences between these structures. Not only that all four designs are instances of tectonism, but moreover all four are lightweight shell structures displaying a similar characteristic organic intricacy. The four pavilions have here been organized into a simple two-by-two matrix. If we read the array as horizontal rows, we can see that the pavilions within each row share color and materiality, namely timber in the first row and carbon fiber in the second row. If we read the array as vertical columns, we see that each column to some extent shares a geometric pattern: in the first column the structures are built up from hexagonal cells, while the second column shows structures constituted through continuous linear elements (Figs. 176–179). It is from such overlapping

Figs. 176–179: ICD/ITKE Research Pavilions, led by Prof. Achim Menges and Prof. Jan Knippers, Stuttgart University 2012–2015

dimensions of contrasts and similitudes that semiological systems can be built up. Each space is distinguished/contrasted via two aspects (materiality and geometry), as well as being affiliated/grouped via these aspects. In this way every space can accumulate several meaning components to establish a complex meaning and nuanced designation.

Here I shall present three design research projects in parametric semiology utilizing characteristic tectonic features that originate from engineering logics. However, the semiology of these projects had not been elaborated with the same complexity and systematicity displayed in the AADRL project shown above. The three designs presented here are a subset of the projects that had been the result of a so-called "option studio" that I had been teaching at Harvard Graduate School of Design in the fall of 2013. My teaching partner was Marc Fornes.[21]

---

21 My teaching assistants were Juan Pablo Ugarte and Jared Ramsdell. Students: Alessandro Boccacci, Conor Coghlan, Mark Eichler, Christopher Esper, Shaoliang Hua, Kayla Lim, Felix Luong, John Morrison, Joseph Ross, Sarkis Sarkisyan, Jie Xie, Weishun Xu, and Juan Yactayo.

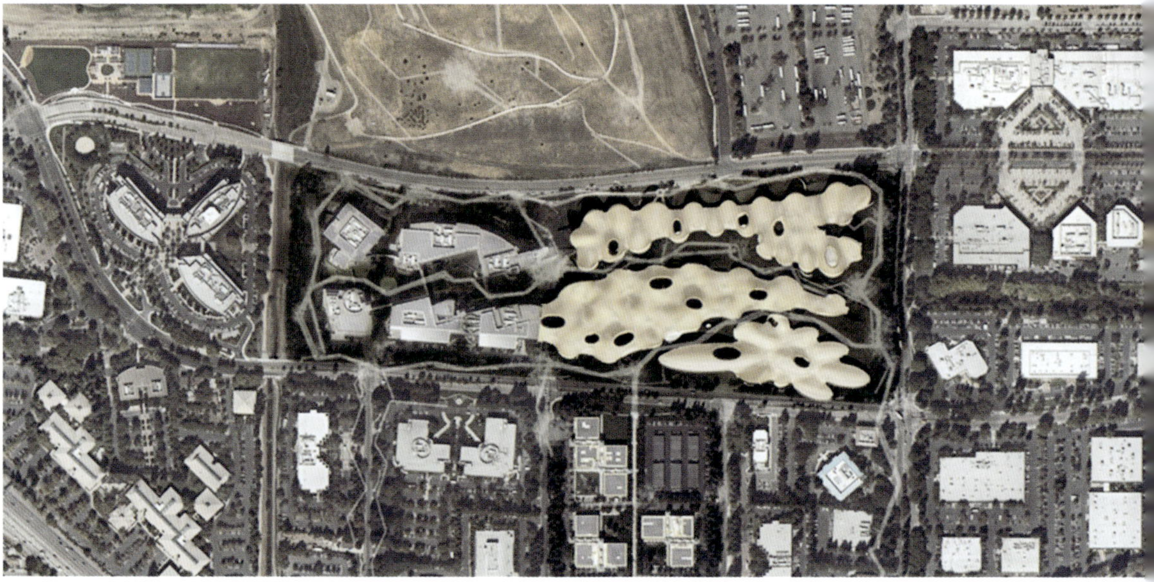

Fig. 180: Active Bending Grid Shells, Conor Coghlan and Shaoliang Hua, Studio Schumacher/Fornes, Harvard Graduate School of Design 2013

The studio brief I put forward read as follows: "Every talented/successful designer adapts to and intervenes intuitively within the spontaneous and historically evolving semiological system of the built environment. The aim of the project brief is to move from an intuitive participation within an evolving semiosis to an explicit design agenda that understands the design of a large-scale architectural complex—like a corporate campus—as an opportunity to design a new, coherent spatio-morphological system of signification. High-performance, creative organizations like Apple, Google or Facebook are the perfect clients for a design approach that aspires to become a global best practice for twenty-first century architecture. Organizations like Apple, Google, or Facebook entail a sufficiently large and complex matrix of social institutions and specific communicative situations, so as to warrant and enable the design of a rich architectural language. The designed campus should be an information-rich, densely articulated environment that orders and encodes the manifold social interactions to be expected and thus facilitates orientation and communication."[22]

The three projects selected here all work with complex aggregations of shell structures. All three projects started with material form-finding experiments with physical models. However, the material

22 For a full documentation of the results see: https://parametricsemiology.wordpress.com.

Figs. 181–184: Active Bending Grid Shells, Conor Coghlan and Shaoliang Hua, Studio Schumacher/Fornes, Harvard Graduate School of Design 2013

processes explored were all rather different, leading to different shell geometries and to different detailed articulations. Each of the different shell systems allows for parametric variation wiithin the constraints of the system. There are scale variations, and variations in terms of proportion. Furthermore, all systems allow for interesting compositional moves like shell nesting, shell intersection, or shell fusions. All three projects started out with finding or developing algorithms that would allow to simulate the material formation processes explored in the physical models, a methodology I brought from the AADRL.

The first project, Active Bending Grid Shells (Fig. 180), took its inspiration from Frei Otto's Mannheim Multihalle. It works with the active bending of timber slats in the formation of grid shells. Special features include soft undulating fusion of shells in aggregations and skylights and courtyards. The cut-outs for the courtyards need to be reinforced by an edge beam and the undulations call for special fan columns to pick up the valleys in the undulating shell formations (Figs. 181–184). (The ground support for these thin grid shells needs to be spread to many support points as load concentrations of the shell must be avoided.)

The second project, Catenary Fields, took its inspiration from Gaudí's hanging models. It works with fields of shells whereby each shell form is being generated by arrays of connected catenary lines (Figs. 185–186). The special feature of this project is that the secondary surface articulations of the catenary shells is constituted by a fractally embedded array of smaller catenary arches, generating apertures for daylight penetration (Figs. 187–189).

Figs. 185–189: Catenary Fields, Alessandro Boccacc Studio Schumacher/ Fornes, Harvard Graduate School of Design 2013

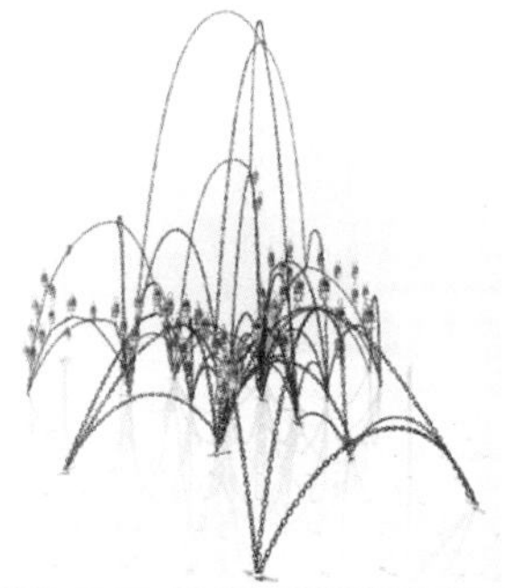

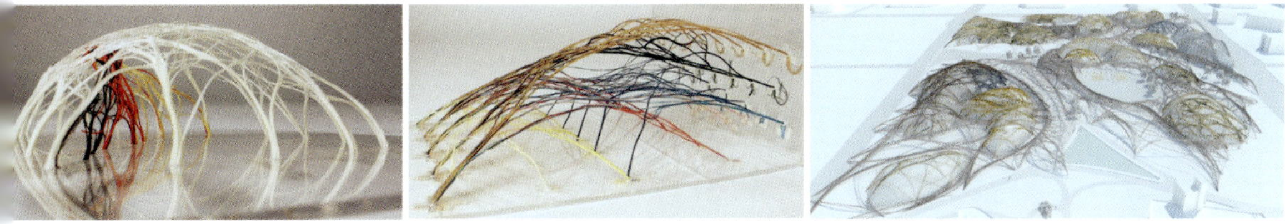

Figs. 190–192: Wool Threads, John Morrison, Studio Schumacher/Fornes, Harvard Graduate School of Design 2013

The third project, Wool Threads, took its inspiration from Frei Otto's experimental wool thread models. These models were originally conceived as material simulations of optimized detour systems for urban path networks. Here, however, they are used to simulate load path networks. The principle here is the bundling up of many thin threads into larger beams in ways that optimize the channeling of loads (Figs. 190–192). The compositional system developed here allows for stacking/nesting of shells as well as for the intersection of shells. The scale and shape of the shells are also varied. Like the other two parametric tectonic systems, this system, too, allows for an adaptive self-organizing optimization of the structural system with respect to diverse outline, height, and support conditions (Figs. 193–195).

Figs. 193–195: Wool Threads, John Morrison, Studio Schumacher/Fornes, Harvard Graduate School of Design 2013

Despite the compelling beauty and rationality of these solutions, a certain difficulty and limitation emerged with all three projects. At the scale of a new Google campus, a certain monotony was hard to avoid, despite all the degrees of freedom in parametric variation. To be sure, the versatility of each of these tectonic systems, and the ability to present internal variation in an otherwise coherent overall expression, was richer than the competing styles of minimalism or high-tech could have offered. Despite this expressive superiority of these projects in the style of tectonism, as single-system schemes, none of the schemes delivered enough conspicuous qualitative variation to meet the requirements of a large corporate campus with so much internal programmatic variation like a Google campus.

From these reflections, the idea of a solution emerged: Ideally, a project as complex and internally differentiated as a Google campus should bring several tectonic systems into play within the same project. Here this would have meant to fuse the three project teams into a single team to explore the juxtaposition or super-imposition of all three tectonic morphologies in a single complex project. This would have avoided the emerging sense of monotony without leading to the formal disintegration of the project. Each of the three schemes, although radically distinct in their ontological constitution, is nevertheless operating from within the same paradigm, namely tectonism, thus working with sufficiently similar principles and values in order to achieve a unified but qualitatively differentiated overall solution.

The traditional way of overcoming monotony in large industrial estates in recent years has been the distribution of the different buildings to different architects, each working in rather unrelated ways, sometimes with incompatible styles. An example of this is the Novartis campus in Basel, Switzerland. In contrast, under the assumption of a unified epochal style like parametricism with a current best-practice subsidiary style like tectonism, this collapse into a collage condition (where unrelated forms collide and create visual chaos) can be avoided. Up to a certain scale a single firm working within the paradigm of tectonism might have sufficient experience and resourcefulness inhouse to generate the required diversity of expression alone. Beyond that scale, e.g., at the scale of urban districts, many architects could come together to generate the richness of expression that gives expression to the richness of the life processes to be facilitated and made transparent within the urban district. However, assuming that parametricism/tectonism has become the hegemonic style of the twenty-first century—and there is no other viable candidate on the horizon—the works of an uncoordinated multiplicity of architectural authors could neverheless forge a unified, coherent urban district.

4.6. The Progression of Styles in Terms of Order and Freedom

The convergence of our discipline to a hegemonic epochal style would allow our urban civilization to avoid the disorienting visual chaos that we witness today everywhere in the world due to the fragmentation of the discipline. A unity of style is thus a condition for the unity of urban expression, which in turn is a precondition to maintain legibility in the face of complexity. However, not any unity suffices here. In the twenty-first century it must be the complex, adaptive, differentiated unity afforded by parametricism and tectonism. Only this style offers the formal resources and computational methodologies that are required to keep up with the contingent process of market driven programmatic self-organization within the city. Parametricism is also the only style capable of expressing the complex synergy relations that exist across the very diverse urban offerings that cluster and connect within the city. Parametricism allows morphologies to resonnate with each other, adapt to each other, formally affiliate with each other. Tectonism in particular allows a further path dependent formation of unique urban identities, based on topographic, climatic, and material conditions.

Parametricism, including tectonism, can draw and exploit the following a powerful analogy: The analogy of unplanned multi-author parametric urbanism with a multispecies ecology. Consider the way the various features and creatures within a natural environment coalesce to create a complex variegated order on the basis of rules—in turn based on the complex interaction of multiple laws of nature—that establish systematic correlations between the various organic and anorganic subsystems that make up a natural landscape. The topography correlates with the path of the river, the river together with topography and sun orientation differentiate the flora and the differentiation of the flora—together with river and topography—shape the differentiation and distribution of the fauna, which in turn impacts back on the flora and thus often also on rivers and even the topography. While thus causality is complex and often circular, correlations and thus inference potentials are being established in all directions, and give information to those who want to navigate such a landscape. The key here is the build-up of correlations and associations (irrespective of the underlying causality). Each new species of plant or animal proliferates according to its own rules of adaptation and survival. For instance, the moss grows differentially on the terraced rock surface in certain shaded slopes, i.e., depending on surface pattern, sun orientation, self-shading rock formation, etc. A population of a certain species of bird then might settle on these slopes accordingly, etc. In the same way parametricism envisions the build-up of a densely layered urban environment via differentiated, rule-based architectural interventions, that are designed via scripts that form the new architectural sub-systems, just like a new species settles into a natural environment. This process delivers rich diversity, yet fully correlated, if designed according to the heuristics of parametricism/tectonism. Each new architect/author can be uniquely creative in inventing and designing the rules/scripts of their project and participate in its own unique way in the build-up of a variegated, information-rich urban order. The analogy also extends to the navigation in rule-based environments: the urbanite's intuitive orientation within a parametric urban environment functions analogous to animal cognition/navigation in a natural environment.

Parametricism, including tectonism, achieves an inversion of architecture's entropy law. Throughout architectural history the required increases in versatility delivered by expansions of design freedoms had to be bought by giving up order. This seemed to be an inevitable trade off: more freedom equals less order. This "entropy law" of historical style progression was only reversed by the advent of parametricism. The techniques of parametricism, and especially tectonism, give a new, powerful ordering capacity to the discipline of architecture, a capacity that delivers a simultaneous enhancement of freedom and order.

If we look at the historical progression of styles we find that during the last 300 years all gains in terms of design freedom and versatility have been achieved at the expense of urban and architectural order, i.e., increases in versatility had to be paid for by a progressive degeneration of architecture's ordering capacity. The increase of the designer's degrees of freedom was established via the enrichment of architecture's formal-compositional repertoire. This increase in freedom/versatility was the paramount criterion of progress in architecture's pursuit of matching the requisite variety of societal complexity. Like the move from classical architecture to modernism, the move from modernism via postmodernism to deconstructivism delivered an expansion of degrees of freedom and versatility (to accommodate a more complex society) that was traded in for a relaxation or rejection of rules of composition, i.e., of means of ordering, and thus a resultant degeneration of the visual order. In the move from classical architecture to modernism symmetry and proportion were given up. In the move from modernism to postmodernism and deconstructivism the order of orthogonality, repetition, balanced asymmetry and the crisp separation of parts/functions was left behind.

Order was progressively eroded. This long trend of a negative correlation of freedom and order can be reversed under the auspices of parametricism. Parametricism—in all its subsidiary styles—offers the simultaneous increase in freedom and order and thus inaugurates a new phase of architectural neg-entropy. Parametricism's radical ontological and methodological innovation translates into a massive leap in both dimensions of architectural progress considered here, i.e., it entails an unprecedented expansion of architecture's compositional freedom and an unprecedented leap in architecture's ordering capacity through the deployment of algorithms.

Parametricism is the first style that delivers further degrees of freedom and versatility in conjunction with a simultaneous increase in its ordering capacity via new compositional rules like affiliations, gradients, and associative logics. In principle all design moves are now rule based and thus with the potential to enhance the visual order and thus legibility of the built environment in the face of an increased complexity. This pertains to all subsidiary styles of parametricism. However, tectonism pulls away from foldism, blobism, and swarmism especially with respect to its ordering capacity. While tectonism delivers yet another expansion of architecture's repertoire for problem solving and articulation, the additional design resources flowing from the utilization of so many cohering logics coming from all the engineering disciplines—structural, environmental, material fabrication—are operating more in the direction of architecture's ordering and cohering capacity than in the direction of an unfettered expansion of the designer's degrees of freedom. In fact, the new expansion of architecture's design repertoire comes along with new constraints. This is why the relevant segment of the graph (Fig. 196) points more upward than forward, although it is fair to presume that a certain net gain in design options or choices is being delivered by the move from swarmism to tectonism.

Fig. 196: Progression of styles: Freedom versus Order

Progression of Styles

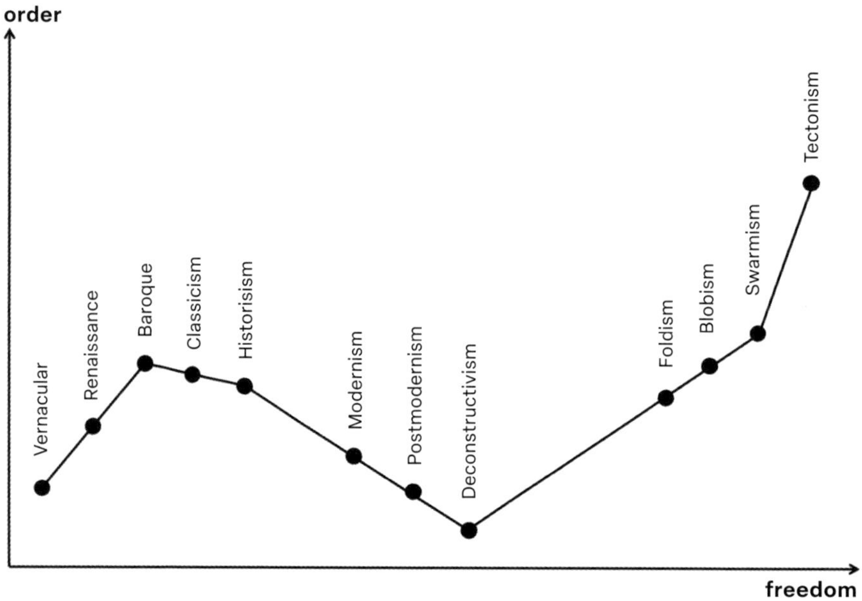

Parametricism, including tectonism, achieves an inversion of architecture's entropy law. Freedom must be bought by giving up order until the techniques of parametricism give a new, powerful ordering capacity to the discipline of architecture, a capacity that delivers a simultaneous enhancement of freedom and order.

In conclusion: The only viable candidate for the next hegemonic epochal style is parametricism/tectonism. Neither a hegemonic postmodernism, nor a hegemonic deconstructivism could overcome the visual chaos that allows the proliferation of differences to collapse into global sameness (white noise). Both postmodernism and deconstructivism operate via collage, i.e., via the unconstrained agglomeration of differences. Deconstructivism can be looked at as the aesthetic sublimation of the urban process of "garbage spill" collage. Tectonism has the capacity to combine an increase in complexity with a simultaneous increase in order, via the principles of lawful differentiation and multi-system correlation. Tectonism can overcome the visual chaos and white noise sameness that laissez faire urbanization produces everywhere. Tectonism holds out the possibility of a free market urbanism that produces an emergent order and local identity in a bottom-up process, i.e., without relying on political or bureaucratic power. The values and methodological principles of tectonism are prone to produce path-dependent, self-amplifying local identities, starting with the given natural features and settlements. Its ethos of contextual affiliation and its ambition to establish or reinforce continuities allows for the development of unique urban identities on the basis of local contexts, topography, climate, etc.

The urban order delivered by tectonism does not rely on the uniform repetition of patterns as modernist urbanism does. In contrast to baroque or Beaux-Arts master plans, the compositions of parametricism and tectonism are inherently open-ended (incomplete) compositions. Their order is relational rather than geometric. They establish order and orientation via the lawful differentiation of fields, via vectors of transformation, as well as via contextual affiliations and subsystem correlations. This neither requires the completion of a figure, nor—in contrast to modernist master plans—the uniform repetition of a pattern. There are always many (in principle infinitely many) creative ways to transform, to affiliate, to correlate. A unique, unpredictable, but recognizable and legible order (which allows for orienting inferences) will emerge, as long as all architects acquire the required skills and create within the new epochal style, paradigm, and ethos that calls for continuities and affiliations, under the critical eye and peer pressure of all colleagues. A hegemonic tectonism thus holds out the prospect of a free market urban order.

Instead of the current global urban condition where all cities and city expansions present the same characterless visual chaos—a condition I have elsewhere called "garbage spill urbanization"—a hegemonic parametricism/tectonism would allow cities to regain a unique character and identity, intuitively recognizable and distinguishable from all other cities. These identities will not be preconceived clichés but will emerge from the conscientious, collective application of rigorously rational designs, based on the principles of tectonism. Although the mere application of these principles would go far in delivering both differentiation and coherence, more can be achieved if the problem of phenomenological and semiological articulation and embedding would become a further explicit agenda and pursuit in each and every project. This can only be achieved if the movement of tectonism takes on this additional congenial task. To steer the movement, and the discipline at large, into this realization and direction is the purpose of this book.

Parametricism, in its latest instantiation as tectonism, is by now manifestly superior to all other styles—without exception mere retro styles—that are still pursued and promoted. This implies that parametricism should sweep the market and put an end to the current pluralism of styles (that resulted from modernism's crisis and) that has been going on for far too long due to ideological inertia. The plurality of styles must make way for a sweeping, universal, i.e., hegemonic parametricism/tectonism, to allow twenty-first-century architecture to finally have, once more, a vital, decisive, transformative impact on the built environment, the way modernism had done in the twentieth century, namely to deliver a total remake of our planet's urban physiognomy.

References

Alberti, Leon Battista, *On the Art of Building in Ten Books*, translated by Joseph Rykwert, Neil Leach, & Robert Tavernor, MIT Press, Cambridge Massachusetts 1988.

Amin, Ash, *Post-Fordism—A Reader*, Blackwell Publishers, Oxford 1994.

Block, Philippe, "Parametricism's Structural Congeniality," *AD Parametricism 2.0—Rethinking Architecture's Agenda for the 21st Century*, editor: H. Castle, guest-edited by Patrik Schumacher, AD Profile #240, March/April 2016.

Blondel, Jacques-Francois, "Course of Architecture, 1771," Harry Francis Malgrave (ed.), *Architectural Theory*, Blackwell Publishing, Oxford 2006.

Boffrand, Germain, *Book of Architecture Containing the General Principles of the Art*, Ashgate Publishing, Aldershot 2003, French original: *Livre d'architecture*, 1745.

Booshan, Shajay, "Upgrading Computational Design," *AD Parametricism 2.0—Rethinking Architecture's Agenda for the 21st Century*, editor: H. Castle, guest-edited by Patrik Schumacher, AD Profile #240, March/April 2016.

Burry, Mark, "Antoni Gaudí and Frei Otto: Essential Precursors to the Parametricism Manifesto," *AD Parametricism 2.0—Rethinking Architecture's Agenda for the 21st Century*, editor: H. Castle, guest-edited by Patrik Schumacher, AD Profile #240, March/April 2016.

Conrads, Ulrich, *Programmes and Manifestos on 20th Century Architecture*, MIT Press, Cambridge Massachusetts 1971.

de Saussure, Ferdinand, *Course in General Linguistics*, Duckworth, 4th edition, London 1995, French original: *Cours de linguistique générale*, Geneva 1916.

Deleuze, Gilles & Guattari, Felix, *A Thousand Plateaus*, The Athlone Press, Minneapolis 1987, French original: *Mille Plateaux*, Paris 1980.

Eco, Umberto, "The Influence of Roman Jakobson on the Development of Semiotics," Martin Krampen et. al. (eds.), *Classics of Semiotics*, Plenum Press, New York 1987.

Fornes, Mark, "The Art of the Prototypical," *AD Parametricism 2.0—Rethinking Architecture's Agenda for the 21st Century*, editor: H. Castle, guest-edited by Patrik Schumacher, AD Profile #240, March/April 2016.

Frampton, Kenneth, *Studies in Tectonic Culture—The Poetics of Construction in Nineteenth and Twentieth Century Architecture*, MIT Press, Cambridge Massachusetts 1995.

Gabo, N. & Pevsner, A., "Basic Principles of Constructivism," Ulrich Conrads, *Programmes and Manifestos on 20th Century Architecture*, MIT Press, Cambridge Massachusetts 1971.

Gandelsonas, Mario, "From Structure to Subject: The Formation of an Architectural Language," *Oppositions* 17, Summer 1979.

Hensel, M. & Menges, A. (eds.), *Morpho-ecologies*, Architectural Association, London 2006.

Hirst, Paul & Zeitlin, Jonathan, *Flexible Specialization Versus Post-Fordism*, Routledge, London 1991.

Huang, X. & Xie, Y.M., *Evolutionary Topology Optimization of Continuum Structures—Methods and Applications*, John Wiley & Sons Ltd., Chichester, United Kingdom 2010.

Huebsch, Heinrich, "In What Style Should We Build?," German original from 1828: *In welchem Style sollen wir bauen?*, excerpt in: Harry Francis Mallgrave (ed.), *Architectural Theory*, Blackwell Publishing, Oxford 2006.

Institute for Lightweight Structures, SFB 230, *Natural Structures—Principles, Strategies, and Models in Architecture and Nature, Proceedings of the II. International Symposium of the Sonderforschungsbereich* 230, Stuttgart 1991.

Jencks, Charles & Baird, George (eds.), *Meaning in Architecture*, George Braziller, New York 1970.

Jencks, Charles, "Semiology and Architecture," Charles Jencks & George Baird (eds.), *Meaning in Architecture*, George Braziller, New York 1970.

Jencks, Charles, *The Language of Post-modern Architecture*, (1st edition 1977), 5th edition, Rizzoli, New York 1987.

Kipnis, Jeffrey, "Towards a New Architecture," *AD Architectural Design*, Profile #102, London 1993.

Laugier, Marc-Antoine, *An Essay on Architecture*, Hennessey & Ingalls, Los Angeles 1977, French original: *Essai sur l'architecture*, 1753.

Leach, N., Turnbull, D., & Williams, C. (eds.), *Digital Tectonics*, Wiley Academy, 2004.

Le Corbusier, *The City of Tomorrow and its Planning*, Dover Publications, New York 1987, translated from French original: *Urbanisme*, Paris 1925.

Le Corbusier, *Towards a New Architecture*, Dover Publications, New York 1986, unaltered republication of English translation of 13th French edition, published by John Rodker, London 1931, French original: *Vers une architecture*, Paris 1923.

Luhmann, Niklas, *Social Systems*, Stanford University Press, California, 1995, German original: *Soziale Systeme: Grundriss einer allgemeinen Theorie*, Frankfurt 1984.

Luhmann, Niklas, *Die Desellschaft der Gesellschaft*, Vols. 1 & 2, Frankfurt am Main, 1998.

Lynn, Greg (ed.), "Folding in Architecture," *AD Architectural Design*, Profile #102, London 1993.

Menges, Achim (ed.), "Material Computation—Higher Integration in Morphogenetic Design," *Architectural Design*, Vol. 82, No. 2, Wiley Academy, London 2012.

Menges, Achim (ed.), "Material Synthesis—Fusing the Physical and the Computational," *Architectural Design*, Vol. 85, No. 5, Wiley Academy, London 2015.

Metcalfe, Ballard, "A Structural Optimization of Félix Candela's Chapel of St. Vincent de Paul in Coyoacán, Mexico City," Princeton University Undergraduate Senior Theses, Civil and Environmental Engineering, United States 2014.

Meyer, Hannes, "bauen," *Bauhaus* Year 2, No. 4, Bauhaus Dessau 1928.

Murray, Robin, "Fordism and Post-Fordism," Stuart Hall & Martin Jacques, *New Times*, London 1989.

Muthesius, Hermann, *Style-Architecture and Building-Art: Transformations of Architecture in the Nineteenth Century and its Present Condition*, University of Chicago Press, Chicago 1994, German original: *Stilarchitektur und Baukunst: Wandlungen der Architektur im XIX. Jahrhundert und ihr heutiger Standpunkt*, Schimmelpfeng, Mülheim-Ruhr 1902.

Naumann, Friedrich, "Die Kunst im Zeitalter der Maschine," *Kunstwart* 17, July 1904.

Norberg-Schulz, Christian, *Architecture: Presence, Language, Place*, Skira Editore, Milan 2000.

Otto, Frei & Rasch, Bodo, *Finding Form—Towards an Architecture of the Minimal*, Edition Axel Menges, Stuttgart 1995.

Peirce, Charles S., *Peirce on Signs—Writings on Semiotics*, University of North Carolina Press, Chapel Hill & London 1991.

Perrault, Claude, *Ordonnance des cinq especes de colonnes selon la method des anciens*, University of Chicago Press, Chicago 1993, French original: 1683.

Pfammatter, Ulrich, *The Making of the Modern Architect and Engineer—The Origins and Development of a Scientific and Industrially Oriented Education*, Birkhaeuser, Basel 2000.

Preziosi, Donald, *Architecture, Language, and Meaning—The Origins of the Built World and its Semiotic Organization*, Mouton Publishers, The Hague 1979.

Preziosi, Donald, *The Semiotics of the Built Environment—An Introduction to Architectonic Analysis*, Indiana University Press, Bloomington 1979.

Rahim, Ali, *Catalytic Formations—Architecture and Digital Design*, Taylor & Francis, New York 2006.

Reiser, Jesse & Umemoto, Nanako, *Atlas of Novel Tectonics*, Princeton Architectural Press, New York 2006.

Schinkel, Karl Friedrich, *Das Architektonische Lehrbuch*, Deutscher Kunstverlag, Munich/Berlin 2001.

Schumacher, Patrik, "Parametricism: A New Global Style for Architecture and Urban Design," Neil Leach (ed.), "AD Digital Cities," *Architectural Design* Vol. 79, No. 4, July/August 2009. Reprinted in: Carpo, Mario, *The Digital Turn in Architecture 1992-2012* (AD Reader).

Schumacher, Patrik, *The Autopoiesis of Architecture, Volume 1: A New Framework for Architecture,* John Wiley & Sons Ltd., London 2010.

Schumacher, Patrik, *The Autopoiesis of Architecture, Volume 2: A New Agenda for Architecture,* John Wiley & Sons Ltd., London 2012.

Schumacher, Patrik, "Tectonics—The Differentiation and Collaboration of Architecture and Engineering," *Bearing Lines—Bearing Surfaces*, Stefan Polonyi, MAI—Museum für Architektur und Ingenieurkunst NRW e.V., Ursula Kleefisch-Jobst et al. (eds.), Edition Axel Menges, Stuttgart/London 2012.

Schumacher, Patrik, "Parametric Semiology—The Design of Information Rich Environments," *Architecture in Formation—On the Nature of Information in Digital Architecture*, Pablo Lorenzo-Eiroa & Aaron Sprecher (eds.), Routledge, Taylor & Francis, New York 2013 (Chinese translation: *Digital 2.0—Urbanism & Architecture* #189–10.2015).

Schumacher, Patrik, "The Congeniality of Architecture and Engineering—The Future Potential and Relevance of Shell Structures in Architecture," *Shell Structures for Architecture—Form Finding and Optimization*, Sigrid Adriaenssens, Philippe Block, Diederik Veenendaal, & Chris Williams (eds.), Routledge, New York 2014.

Schumacher, Patrik, "Tectonic Articulation—Making Engineering Logics Speak," *AD 04/2014, Future Details of Architecture*, guest-edited by Mark Garcia, July/August 2014.

Schumacher, Patrik, "Design Parameters to Parametric Design," *The Routledge Companion for Architecture Design and Practice: Established and Emerging Trends*, Mitra Kanaani & Dak Kopec (eds.), Routledge, Taylor & Francis, New York 2016.

Schumacher, Patrik, "Introduction to Parametricism 2.0—Gearing Up to Impact the Global Built Environment," *AD Parametricism 2.0—Rethinking Architecture's Agenda for the 21st Century*, editor: H. Castle, guest-edited by Patrik Schumacher, AD Profile #240, March/April 2016.

Schumacher, Patrik, "Advancing Social Functionality via Agent-Based Parametric Semiology," *AD Parametricism 2.0—Rethinking Architecture's Agenda for the 21st Century*, editor: H. Castle, guest-edited by Patrik Schumacher, AD Profile #240, March/April 2016.

Schumacher, Patrik, "Hegemonic Parametricism Delivers a Market-Based Urban Order," *AD Parametricism 2.0—Rethinking Architecture's Agenda for the 21st Century*, editor: H. Castle, guest-edited by Patrik Schumacher, AD Profile #240, March/April 2016.

Schumacher, Patrik, "Style—Aligning Architectural Styles with Societal Epochs," *The Architectural Review* 120 (120th anniversary issue), 1437, December 2016/January 2017.

Schumacher, Patrik, "Tectonism in Architecture, Design and Fashion—Innovations in Digital Fabrication as Stylistic Drivers," *AD 3D-Printed Body Architecture*, guest-edited by Neil Leach & Behnaz Farahi, *Architectural Design*, Profile #250, November/December 2017, 06/Vol 87/2017.

Schumacher, Patrik, Zheng Lei, "From Typology to Topology: Social, Spatial, and Structural," *Architectural Journal*, No. 590, 2017/11, Source journal for Chinese scientific and technical papers and citations; Sponsor: The Architectural Society of China, Chief editor: Cui Kai.

Schumacher, Patrik, "The Progress of Geometry as Design Resource," *Log*, Summer 2018, Issue on Geometry.

Schumacher, Patrik, "DIGITAL—The 'Digital' in Architecture and Design," *AA Files* No. 76, Architectural Association, London 2019.

Schumacher, Patrik, "Parametricism: The Next Decade," *a+u Architecture+Urbanism* 2020:04, No. 595, Feature: Computational Discourses.

Schumacher, Patrik, "Social Performativity: Architecture's Contribution to Societal Progress," in: *The Routledge Companion to Paradigms of Performativity in Design and Architecture: Using Time to Craft an Enduring, Resilient and Relevant Architecture*, ed. Mitra Kanaani, Routledge, Taylor & Francis, New York & London 2020.

Schwab, Klaus, "The Fourth Industrial Revolution," World Economic Forum, 2016.

Semper, Gottfried, *Style in the Technical and Tectonic Arts, or Practical Aesthetics*, Getty Publications, Los Angeles 2004, German original: *Der Stil in den Technischen und Tektonischen Kuensten; oder Praktische Aesthetik: Ein Handbuch fuer Techniker*, Kuenstler und Kunstfreunde, Vol.1 Verlag fuer Kunst und Wissenschaft, Frankfurt am Main 1860; Vol. 2 Bruckmann Verlag, Munich 1863.

Semper, Gottfried, "Ueber Baustile (On Architectural Styles)," in: Gottfried Semper, *Wissenschaft, Industrie und Kunst*, Neue Bauhausbuecher, Florian Kupferberg, Mainz/Berlin 1966.

Spyropoulos, Theodore, *Adaptive Ecologies: Correlated Systems of Living*, Architectural Association, London 2013.

Steele, Brett (ed.), *Corporate Fields—New Office Environments by the AADRL*, AADRL Documents 1, AA Publications, Architectural Association School of Architecture, London 2005.

Viollet le Duc, E. E., *Lectures on Architecture*, 2 vols (1863, 1872), translated by B. Bucknall (1877, 1881), Dover Publications, New York, 1987.

Vrachliotis, G. (ed.), *Frei Otto—Denken in Modellen*, Specter Books, Leipzig 2016.

Woodbury, Robert, *Elements of Parametric Design*, Routledge, London/New York 2010.

Yuan, Philip, "Parametric Regionalism," *AD Parametricism 2.0—Rethinking Architecture's Agenda for the 21st Century*, editor: H. Castle, guest-edited by Patrik Schumacher, AD Profile #240, March/April 2016.

Yuan, P., Menges, A., & Leach, N. (eds.), *Digital Fabrication*, Tongji University Press, Shanghai 2018.

Image Credits

All images are supplied courtesy Patrik Schumacher, with exceptions noted for the following pages. (Figures are depicted left to right, top to bottom, on the main pages.)

©in3d 124 (Figs. 152, 154)

AADRL 80

Iwan Baan 34 (Fig. 9)

Virgile Simon Bertrand 58–59, 100–101

Hélène Binet 32–33, 68 (Fig. 35)

Philippe Block (BRG) 87 (Fig. 84)

BRG 87 (Fig. 85)

Richard Bryant 42 (Fig. 17)

Daniel Chung 68 (Fig. 34: drone image)

Alessandro Dell'endice 124 (Figs. 153, 155)

Ivan Dupont 2–3, 98

Hans Georg Esch 104 (Fig. 111)

Julian Faulhaber/ VG Bild-Kunst/Copyright Agency 68 (Fig. 36)

Luke Hayes 75, 76 (Fig. 52, 54, 55), 77, 78–79, 121

Hufton + Crow 68 (Fig. 33), 91 (Fig. 93), 92–93, 94 (Figs. 98–100), 95, 96–97, 104 (Fig. 112), 106–107, 109 (Figs. 118–120), 155, 160

Werner Huthmacher 34 (Figs. 5–8)

Delfino Sisto Legnani + Marco Cappelletti 123

Naaro 125 (Fig. 157), 126–127

Odico 120 (Fig. 139)

Sergio Pirrone 116 (Figs. 131–133), 171

RoboFold 116 (Figs. 129, 130)

Mirren Rosie 128 (Fig. 159)

Stratasys 122 (Fig. 144)

Alejandro Vazquez 43 (Fig. 19)

Zaha Hadid Architects 26 (Figs. 3, 4), 43 (Fig. 18), 44 (Fig. 20), 45 (Fig. 22), 46–47, 52–53, 54, 62, 64–65, 81, 82, 83, 85 (Figs. 78, 79, 80), 88, 94 (Figs. 94–97), 108 (Figs. 114–117), 110, 111, 112–113, 116 (Fig. 128), 120 (Fig. 138), 122 (Fig. 143, 145), 124 (Figs. 148–151), 125 (Fig. 156), 130, 152

Xia Zhi 86

Project Credits

Mountain Train, Innsbruck, Austria 2004–2007

Design Zaha Hadid & Patrik Schumacher

Project architect Thomas Vietzke

Design team Jens Borstelmann, Markus Planteu

Production team Caroline Andersen, Makakrai Suthadarat, Marcela Spadaro, Anneka Wagener, Adriano di Gionnis, Peter Pichler, Susann Berggren

Façade planning Pagitz Metalltechnik GMBH

Contractors *[Total]* Strabag AG; *[Engines & cables]* Leitner GmbH

Planning advisors ILF Beratende Ingenieure ZT, Gessellschaft GmbH, Malojer Baumanagement GmbH

Structural engineers *[Roof]* Bollinger Grohmann Schneider; *[Concrete base]* Baumann & Obholzer ZT_GmbH

Bridge engineer ILF Beratende Ingenieure ZT, Gessellschaft GmbH

Lighting Zumbotel Lighting GmbH

Dongdaemon Design Centre plaza and park, Seoul, Korea 2007–2014

Design Zaha Hadid & Patrik Schumacher

Project leaders Eddie Can, Chiu-Fai

Project managers Craig Kiner, Charles Walker

Project team Kaloyan Erevinov, Martin Self, Hooman Talebi, Carlos S. Martinez, Camiel Weijenberg, Florian Goscheff, Maaike Hawinkels, Aditya Chandra, Andy Chang, Arianna Russo, Ayat Fadaifard, Josias Hamid, Shuojiong Zhang, Natalie Koerner, Jae Yoon Lee, Federico Rossi, John Klein, Chikara Inamura, Alan Lu

Competition team Kaloyan Erevinov, Paloma Gormley, Hee Seung Lee, Kelly Lee, Andres Madrid, Deniz Manisali, Kevin McClellan, Claus Voigtmann, Maurits Fennis

Engineers *[Structural, services; lighting & acoustics consultant]* Arup; *[Landscape architect]* Gross Max; *[Façade consultant]* Group 5F; *[Geometry consultant]* Evolute; *[Quantity surveyor]* Davis Langdon & Everest

Local architect Samoo Architects

Local consultants *[Structural]* Postech; *[Mechanical]* Samoo Mechanical Consulting (SMC); *[Electrical & telecommunications]* Samoo TEC; *[Façade]* M&C; *[Civil]* Saegil Engineering & Consulting; *[Landscape]* Dong Sim Won; *[Fire]* Korean Fire Protection Engineering; *[Lighting]* Huel Lighting Design; *[Quantity surveyor]* Kyoung Won; *[Cultural asset]* Josun *[Acoustics]* OSD; *[Noise/vibration]* RMS Technology; *[Energy analytics]* Daeil ENC; *[Maintenance]* Doall CMC; *[Environmental impact]* Soosung Engineering; *[Planning permission]* Sewon P&D

Phaeno Science Center, Wolfsburg, Germany 2000–2005

Architects Zaha Hadid Architects & Mayer Bährle Freie Architekten BDA (Germany)

Design Zaha Hadid & Patrik Schumacher, with Christos Passas

Project architect Christos Passas

Assistant project architect Sara Klomps

Project team Sara Klomps, Gernot Finselbach, David Salazar, Helmut Kinzler

Competition team Christos Passas, Janne Westermann, Chris Dopheide, Stanley Lau, Eddie Can, Yoash Oster, Jan Hubener, Caroline Voet

Contributors Silvia Forlati, Guenter Barczik, Lida Charsouli, Marcus Liermann, Kenneth Bostock, Enrico Kleinke, Constanze Stinnes, Liam Young, Chris Dopheide, Barbara Kuit, Niki Neerpasch, Markus Dochantschi

Mayer Bährle architects *[Project architects]* Rene Keuter, Tim Oldenburg; *[Project team]* Sylvia Chiarappa, Stefan Hoppe, Andreas Gaiser, Roman Bockemühl, Annette Finke, Stefanie Lippardt, Marcus Liermann, Jens Hecht, Christoph Volkmar

Structural engineers *[Adams Kara Taylor (United Kingdom)]* Hanif Kara (Principal), Paul Scott (Project engineer); *[Tokarz Freirichs Leipold (Germany)]* Lothar Leipold, Prof. Bernhard Tokarz

Services engineers NEK (Germany); Buro Happold (Berlin, London)

Cost consultant Hanscomb GmbH (Germany)

Lighting consultants Fahlke & Dettmer (Germany); Office for Visual Interaction (United States)

Brisbane Residential Tower, Queensland, Australia 2014

Design Zaha Hadid & Patrik Schumacher

Project director Michele Pasca di Magliano

Project associate Maurizio Meossi

Project architect Rafael Contreras

Project team Subharthi Guha, Arya Safavi, Cristina Capanna, Veronica Erspamer, Brad Holt, Stefano Paiocchi, Megan Burke, Michael Rogers, Paola Salcedo, Andrew Haas, Gaganjit Singh, Natasha Gill, Grace Chung, Luca Ruggeri, David Fogliano, Juan Camilo Mogollon, Effie Kuan, Andrea Balducci Caste, Domenico Di Francesco, Sobitha Ravichandran, Demetris Alexiou, Monir Karimi, Eleni Mente

Structural engineer Hyder Consulting

Project consultants *[Building services engineer]* EMF Griffiths; *[Local architect]* Conrad Gargett Riddel; *[Quantity surveyor]* Rider Levett Bucknall; *[Façade consultant]* AECOM; *[Landscape designer]* Form; *[Civil engineer]* Brown Consulting; *[Planning consultant]* Wolter Consulting Group; *[Traffic engineer]* TTM Consulting Pty Ltd; *[Acoustics consultant]* Acousticworks

Qingdao Cultural Centre, China 2013

Design Zaha Hadid & Patrik Schumacher

Project directors Nils Fischer, Shao-wei Huang

Project architect Sebastian Andia

Design team Ashwin Shah, Chang Cui, Chao Wei, Ho-ping Hsia, Konstantinos Mouratidis, MengChan Tang, Mu Ren, Nicholette Chan, Suryansh Chandra, Yue Shi, Yung-Chieh Huang

Museum consultant Lord Cultural Resources

Performance consultant Anne Minors Performance Consultants

Engineer *[Structural, façade, sustainability, environmental, & lighting]* Buro Happold

Presidential Palace, Algiers, Algeria 2011–2017

Design Zaha Hadid & Patrik Schumacher

Project director Charles Walker

Project architects Hussam Chakouf, Stephane Vallotton

Architectural team Nassim Eshagi, Nils Fischer, Reda Kessanti, Leonid Krykhtin, Bechara Malkoun, Marie-Perrine Placais, Joris Powels, Frenji Koshy, Zohra Rougab, Elena Scripelliti, Michael Sims, Armando Solano, Stephane Vallotton, Mark Winnington, Fulvio Wirz, Lei Zheng

ZHA CODE team Shajay Booshan, Mostafa El Sayed, Suryansh Chandra, David Reeves

Consultants *[Engineering & cost]* Dar Al-Handasah; *[Structural engineering]* AKT II; *[Landscaping]* Gross Max; *[Façade]* Newtecnic

Lilas, Serpentine Gallery, London, United Kingdom 2007

Design Zaha Hadid & Patrik Schumacher

Project architect Kevin McClellan

Coordinator Harriet Warden

Structural engineering Arup

Steel fabrication Sheetfabs Ltd

Membrane fabrication Base Structures Ltd

Lighting Zumtobel Lighting GmbH

Serpentine North Gallery, Hyde Park, London, United Kingdom, 2009–2013

Design Zaha Hadid & Patrik Schumacher

Project director Charles Walker

Project leads *[Phase 1]* Ceyhun Baskin, Inanc Eray; *[Phase 2]* Thomas Vietzke, Jens Borstelmann; *[Phase 3]* Fabian Hecker

Project team *[Phase 2]* Torsten Broeder, Timothy Schreiber, Laymon Thaung, David Campos, Suryansh Chandra, Matthew Hardcastle, Dillon Lin, Marina Duran Sancho, Jianghai Shen; *[Phase 3]* Torsten Broeder, Anat Stern, Timothy Schreiber, Marcela Spadaro, Inanc Eray, Ceyhun Baskin, Elke Presser, Claudia Wulf; *[Restaurant mise-en-scène & gift shop]* Melodie Leung, Maha Kutay, Claudia Glas-Dorner, Evgeniya Yatsyuk, Kevin Sheppard, Carine Posner, Maria Leni Popovici, Loulwa Bohsali, Karine Yassine, Steve Blaess

Consultants *[Conservation architects]* Liam O'Connor Architects, *[Lighting]* Isometrix (London); *[Structural, services, & fire]* Arup; *[Kitchen]* Sefton Horn Winch; *[Planning]* DP9; *[Project management]* Rise; *[Cost]* Gleeds

Construction *[Contracts administrator]* Gleeds; *[Glazing]* OAG Optima; *[Seating manufacturer]* Alias; *[Kitchen/bar & table manufacturer]* Stage One; *[Restaurant consultant]* Nick Lander

Mathematics Gallery, Science Museum, London, United Kingdom 2014–2016

Design Zaha Hadid & Patrik Schumacher

ZHA project director Charles Walker

ZHA project senior associate Bidisha Sinha

ZHA project associate Shajay Bhooshan

ZHA project team Vishu Bhooshan, Henry Louth, David Reeves, Nhan Vo, Mattia Santi, Sai Prateik Bhasgi, Karthikeyan Arunachalam, Tommaso Casucci, Marko Margeta, Filippo Nassetti, Mostafa El Sayed, Suryansh Chandra, Ming Cheong, Carlos Parraga-Botero, Ilya Pereyaslavtsev, Ramon Weber

Consultants *[Structural, MEP, & lighting]* Arup; *[Project manager]* Lendlease; *[CDM & cost]* Gardiner & Theobald

Construction team *[Main construction]* Paragon; *[Bench fabricator]* ODICO; *[Flooring]* Bolidt; *[Showcases]* Reier

Tokyo 2020 Olympic Stadium, Japan 2014

Design Zaha Hadid & Patrik Schumacher

Project directors Jim Heverin, Cristiano Ceccato

Project architect Paulo Flores

Design core team Rafael Contreras, Antonio Monserrat, Fernando Poucell, Irene Guerra, Junyi Wang, Karoly Markos

Tokyo support team Yoshi Uchiyama, Ben Kikkawa

Candela Revisited, Beijing, China 2013

Design Patrik Schumacher, Shajay Bhooshan, Philipp Ostermaier, Mostafa El Sayed, Suryansh Chandra, Saman Saffarian, Vishu Bhooshan

Coordination & execution Satoshi Ohashi, Feng Lin, Jingwen Yang, Xuexin Duan

Engineering *[Bollinger Grohmann Schneider (Vienna)]* Robert Vierlinger, Moritz Heimrath, Clemens Preisinger, Arne Hofmann

Fabrication *[Cabr Technology Co., Ltd. (Beijing)]* Congzhen, Xiao Tao Song, Feng Liu, Hui Kong

KnitCandela, Mexico City, Mexico

Design *[ZHA CODE]* Filippo Nassetti, Marko Margeta, David Reeves, Leo Beiling, Federico Borello, Henry David Louth, Vishu Bhooshan, Shajay Bhooshan, Patrik Schumacher

Engineering *[Block Research Group (BRG)/ETH Zürich]* Mariana Popescu, Matthias Rippmann, Lex Reiter (Institute for Biomechanics, ETH Zürich), Andrew Liew, Tom Van Mele, Robert Flatt (Institute for Biomechanics, ETH Zürich), Philippe Block

Architecture extrapolated (R-Ex) Horacio Bibiano Vargas, José Manuel Diaz Sánchez, Asunción Zúñiga, Agustín Lozano Álvarez, Miguel Juárez Antonio, Filiberto Juárez Antonio, Daniel Piña, Daniel Celin, Carlos Axel Pérez Cano, José Luis Naranjo Olivares, Everardo Hernandez, Alicia Nahmad Vázquez

VOLU Dining Pavilion, Design Miami, United States 2015

Design Zaha Hadid & Patrik Schumacher

Design team Shajay Bhooshan, Henry Louth, David Reeves, Maha Kutay, Woody Yao

Installation coordinator Ilya Pereyaslavtsev

Animation David Reeves, Filippo Nasetti, Tommaso Casucci, Ilya Pereyaslavtsev

Product geometry developer Benjamin Koren (One to One)

Fabricator Ackermann

Beijing Daxing International Airport, China 2014–2019

Design (ZHA) Zaha Hadid & Patrik Schumacher

Project directors (ZHA) Cristiano Ceccato, Charles Walker, Mouzhan Majidi

Project design director (ZHA) Paulo Flores

Project architect (ZHA) Lydia Kim

Project coordinators (ZHA) Eugene Leung, Shao-Wei Huang

Project team (ZHA) Uli Blum, Antonio Monserrat, Alberto Moletto, Sophie Davison, Carolina Lopez-Blanco, Shaun Farrell, Junyi Wang, Ermis Chalvatzis, Rafael Contreras, Michael Grau, Fernando Poucell, Gerry Cruz, Filipa Gomez, Kyla Farrell, Natassa Lianou, Teoman Ayas, Peter Logan, Yun Zhang, Karoly Markos, Irene Guerra

Beijing team (ZHA) Satoshi Ohashi, Rita Lee, Yang Jingwen, Lillie Liu, Juan Liu

Local design institutes Beijing Institute of Architectural Design (Group) Co. Ltd (BIAD), China Airport Construction Company

Consortium team (competition stage) Pascall+Watson, BuroHappold Engineering, Mott MacDonald, EC Harris Consultants, McKinsey & Company, Dunnett Craven, Triagonal, Logplan, Sensing Places, SPADA

Security system & baggage systems design China IPPR International Engineering Co. Ltd.

Information & weak power systems design China Electronics Engineering Design Institute + Civil Aviation Electronic Technology Co. Ltd.; **Fire performance design** Arup; **Public art** Central Academy of Fine Arts; **Green technology** Beijing TsingHua TongHeng Urban Planning & Design Institute **BIM design** DTree Ltd.; **Architecture façade** XinShan Curtainwall Ltd., Beijing Institute of Architectural Design (Group) Co. Ltd (BIAD) (Complex Structure Division); **Metro system** Lea+Elliott; **Lighting** Gala Lighting Design Studio; **Identification/signage system** East Sign Design & Engineering Co. Ltd. (East); **Landscape** Beijing Institute of Architectural Design (Group) Co. Ltd (BIAD) (Landscape Design Division)

One Thousand Museum, Miami, United States 2012–2020

Design Zaha Hadid & Patrik Schumacher

Project director Chris Lepine

Project team Alessio Costantino, Martin Pfleger, Oliver Bray, Theodor Wender, Irena Predalic, Celina Auterio, Carlota Boyer

Competiton team Sam Saffarian, Eva Tiedemann, Brandon Gehrke, Cynthia Du, Grace Chung, Aurora Santana, Olga Yatsyuk

Local architect O'Donnell Dannwolf & Partners

Engineering *[Structural]* DeSimone Consulting Engineers; *[MEP]* HNGS Consulting Engineers; *[Civil]* Terra Civil Engineering

Landscape Enea Garden Design

Fire protection SLS Consulting Inc.

Vertical transportation Lerch Bates Inc.

Wind tunnel consultant RWDI Consulting Engineers & Scientists

Morpheus Hotel & Resort at City of Dreams, Macau, China, 2013–2018

Design Zaha Hadid & Patrik Schumacher

ZHA project directors Viviana Muscettola, Michele Pasca di Magliano

ZHA façade director Paolo Matteuzzi

ZHA project architects Michele Salvi, Bianca Cheung, Maria Loreto Flores, Clara Martins

ZHA project team Miron Mutyaba, Milind Khade, Pierandrea Angius, Massimo Napoleoni, Stefano Iacopini, Davide Del Giudice, Luciano Letteriello, Luis Migue Samanez, Cyril Manyara, Alvin Triestanto, Muhammed Shameel, Goswin Rothenthal, Santiago Fernandez-Achury, Vahid Eshraghi, Melika Aljukic

ZHA interiors team Daniel Fiser, Thomas Sonder, Daniel Coley, Yooyeon Noh, Jinqi Huang, Mirta Bilos, Alexander Kuroda, Gaganjit Singh, Marina Martinez, Shajay Bhooshan, Henry Louth, Filippo Nassetti, David Reeves, Marko Gligorov, Neil Rigden, Milica Pihler-Mirjanic, Grace Chung, Mario Mattia, Mariagrazia Lanza

ZHA concept team Viviana Muscettola, Tiago Correia, Clara Martins, Maria Loreto Flores, Victor Orive, Danilo Arsic, Inês Fontoura, Fabiano Costinanza, Rafael Gonzalez, Muhammed Shameel

Executive architect Leigh & Orange (Hong Kong)

Local architect CAA City Planning & Engineering Consultants (Macau)

Structural engineering Buro Happold International (London/Hong Kong)

M&E engineering J. Roger Preston

Façade engineering Buro Happold International (Hong Kong)

Third-party reviewer Rolf Jensen & Associates

Other interior designers *[Guestrooms, L01 VIP lobby; L03 spa & gym; L40 pool deck & pool villas]* Remedios Studio (Hong Kong); *[L02 Gaming areas; Li Ying restaurant; L42 gaming salons]* Westar Architects International; *[L03 Alain Ducasse restaurant]* Jouin Manku; *[L30 executive lounge]* MC Design; *[Back-of-house areas]* Leigh & Orange, Macau

Consultants *[Quantity surveyor]* WT Partnership (Hong Kong); *[Lighting]* Isometrix (London/Hong Kong); *[Fire engineer]* Arup (Hong Kong); *[Acoustics consultant]* Shen Milson & Wilke (Hong Kong); *[Traffic engineer]* MVA (Hong Kong)

King Abdullah Petroleum Studies & Research Centre (KAPSARC), Riyadh, Saudi Arabia 2009–2017

Design Zaha Hadid & Patrik Schumacher

Project directors Lars Teichmann, Charles Walker

Design director DaeWha Kang

Project site team *[Site associate]* John Simpson, Alejandro Diaz, Anas Younes, Annarita Papeschi, Aritz Moriones, Ayca Vural Cutts, Carlos Parraga-Botero, Javier Rueda, Malgorzata Kowalczyk, Michal Wojtkiewicz, Monika Bilska, Sara Criscenti, Stella Dourtme

Project leaders *[Research center]* Fabian Hecker; *[Conference center]* Michael Powers; *[Library]* Brian Dale/Henning Hansen; *[Musalla/IT center]* Fulvio Wirz; *[Façades/2D documentation]* Elizabeth Bishop; *[Master plan]* Saleem A. Jalil/Maria Rodero; *[Interiors]* Lisamarie Ambia/Judith Wahle; *[2D documentation]* Bozana Komljenovic; *[Specifications]* John Randle; *[3D documentation coordinator]* John Szlachta

Project team Adrian Krezlik, Alexander Palacio, Amdad Chowdhury, Amit Gupta, Andres Arias Madrid, Britta Knobel, Camiel Weijenberg, Carine Posner, Claire Cahill, Claudia Glas-Dorner, DaChun Lin, Daniel Fiser, Daniel Toumine, David Doody, David Seeland, Deniz Manisali, Ebru Simsek-Lenk, Elizabeth Keenan, Evan Erlebacher, Fernanda Mugnaini, Garin O'Aivazian, Giorgio Radojkovic, Inês Fontoura, Jaimie-Lee Haggerty, Jeremy Tymms, Julian Jones, Jwalant Mahadevwala, Lauren Barclay, Lauren Mishkind, Mariagrazia Lanza, Melike Altinisik, Michael Grau, Michael McNamara, Mimi Halova, MohammadAli Mirzaei, Mohammed Reshdan, Muriel Boselli, MyungHo Lee, Nahed Jawad, Natacha Viveiros, Navvab Taylor, Neil Vyas, Nicola McConnell, Pedro Sanchez, Prashanth Sridharan, Roxana Rakhshani, Saahil Parikh, Sara Saleh, Seda Zirek, Shaju Nanukuttan, Shaun Farrell, Sophie Davison, Sophie Le Bienvenu, Stefan Brabetz, Steve Rea, Suryansh Chandra, Talenia Phua Gajardo, Theodor Wender, Yu Du

Competition design team Lisamarie Ambia, Monika Bilska, Martin Krcha, Maren Klasing, Kelly Lee, Johannes Schafelner, Judith Schafelner, Ebru Simsek, Judith Wahle, Hee Seung Lee, Clara Martins, Anat Stern, Daniel Fiser, Thomas Sonder, Kristina Simkeviciute, Talenia Phua Gajardo, Erhan Patat, Dawna Houchin, Jwalant Mahadevwala

Consultants *[Engineering]* Arup; *[Interior design]* Woods Bagot; *[Landscape design]* Gross Max; *[Lighting design]* OVI; *[Catering & kitchen design]* Eastern Quay and GWP; *[Exhibition design event]* Artwork International Art Consultants; *[Branding & signage]* Elmwood and Bright 3D; *[Library consulting]* Tribal; *[Cost & design project management]* Davis Langdon

Central Bank of Iraq, Baghdad 2011–2022

Design Zaha Hadid & Patrik Schumacher

Project director Jim Heverin

Project associate Sara Klomps

Project architect Victor Orive

Project team Cynthia Du, Danilo Arsic, Electra Mikelides, Fabiano Continanza, Inês Fontoura, Juan Estrada Gomez, Maria Rodero, Ming Cheong, Mohamed Al-Jubori, Muriel Boselli, Osbert So, Peter Irmscher, Rafael Gonzalez, Renee Gao, Sara Criscenti, Thomas Frings

Project team *[DD Phase]* Ana Cajiao, Andy Summers, Daghan Cam, Danilo Arsic, Electra Mikelides, Fabiano Continanza, Ganesh Nimmala, George King, Inês Fontoura, Lisa Curran, Maria Rodero, Ming Cheong, Mohamed Al-Jubori, Monica Jarpa, Rafael Gonzalez; *[SD Phase]* Ana Cajiao, Andy Summers, Danilo Arsic, Electra Mikelides, Fabiano Continanza, George King, Inês Fontoura, Mohamed Al-Jubori, Rafael Gonzalez, Sophie Davison

Concept team Charles Walker, Danilo Arsic, Fabiano Continanza, Inês Fontoura, Rafael Gonzalez, Tiago Correia, Victor Orive

Local architect/architect of record Dijlah Consulting Architects & Engineers

Engineers *[Structural]* AKT II (London); *[Services]* Max Fordham (London); *[Façade]* Newtecnic (London)

Office space planning AECOM (London)

Cost & facilities management Davis Langdon, an AECOM Company (London)

Security & logistics consultant Arup Security (London)

Fire & life safety Exova Warringtonfire (London)

Landscape architect Gross Max (Edinburgh)

Constructability A2 Project Management (London)

Catering consultant Keith Winton Design

Exhibition design Event Communications (London)

Arum, Venice Architecture Biennale 2012

Design Zaha Hadid & Patrik Schumacher

Computational design team Shajay Bhooshan, Saman Saffarian, Suryansh Chandra, Mostafa El Sayed

Structural engineering Rasti Bartek (Buro Happold)

Material & fabrication technology Gregory Epps (RoboFold)

With support from Permasteelisa Spa ARTE & Partners

Science Museum Benches, London, United Kingdom 2014–2016

Design Zaha Hadid & Patrik Schumacher

Design team Shajay Bhooshan, Henry David Louth, David Reeves, Vishu Bhooshan

Coordination & execution Charles Walker, Bidisha Sinha, Ming Cheong, Carlos Parraga-Botera, Paragon Graham Sage

Fabrication ODICO Construction Robotics, Asbjørn Søndergaard, Anders Bundsgaard, Hicon A/S

Thallus, Milan Design Week 2017

Design Zaha Hadid Architects, Patrik Schumacher

ZHA CODE design team Shajay Bhooshan, Henry David Louth, Marko Margeta

Project managers Maha Kutay, Woody Yao, Manon Janssens

Primary sponsor OIKOS

Contributors *[Robotic additive manufacturing]* AiBuild; *[Robotic formworks]* Odico Formwork Robotics; *[Metal works]* Armadillo Engineering

ACADIA 3D Printed Chair 2014

Design Zaha Hadid & Patrik Schumacher

Design team Shajay Bhooshan, Mostafa El Sayed, Vishu Bhooshan, Maha Kutay, Woody Yao

Fabrication design & 3D printing coordination Mostafa El Sayed, Vishu Bhooshan, Shajay Bhooshan

Topology optimization Altair, Ajith Narayanan, Sam Patten, Michal Stefuca

3D printing Stratasys, Naomi Kaempfer, Boris Belocon, Keren Ludomirski-Zait, Charles Evans

Nagami Chairs: Rise, Bow 2018

Design Patrik Schumacher

Design team Sebastian Andia

Production (3D printing) & promotion Nagami

Striatus Bridge, Venice Architecture Biennale 2021

Design Patrik Schumacher; *[ZHA CODE]* Shajay Bhooshan, Jianfei Chu, Vishu Bhooshan, Henry David Louth; *[Block Research Group (BRG)/ETH Zürich]* Alessandro Dell'Endice, Tom Van Mele, Philippe Block

Structural engineering *[Block Research Group (BRG)/ETH Zürich]* Alessandro Dell'Endice, Tom Van Mele, Sam Bouten, Philippe Block

Fabrication design *[Block Research Group (BRG)/ETH Zürich]* Shajay Bhooshan, Alessandro Dell'Endice, Tom Van Mele, Sam Bouten, Chaoyu Du; *[ZHA CODE]* Vishu Bhooshan, Philip Singer, Tommaso Casucci

3D concrete printing *[In3D]* Johannes Megens, Georg Grasser, Sandro Sanin, Nikolas Janitsch, Janos Mohacsi

Concrete material development *[Holcim]* Christian Blachier, Marjorie Chantin-Coquard, Helene Lombois-Burger, Francis Steiner; *[LafargeHolcim Spain]* Benito Carrion, Jose Manuel Arnau

Assembly & construction *[Bürgin Creations]* Theo Bürgin, Semir Mächler, Calvin Graf; *[Block Research Group (BRG)/ETH Zürich]* Alessandro Dell'Endice, Tom Van Mele

Logistics *[Block Research Group (BRG)/ETH Zürich]* Alessandro Dell'Endice, Tom Van Mele; *[Holcim Switzerland & Italy]* Michele Alverd; *[LafargeHolcim Spain]* Ricardo de Pablos, José Luis Romero

Additional partners *[CNC timber formwork]* Ackermann GmbH; *[Site measurements]* L2F Architettura; *[Steel supports]* Pletscher; *[Laser-cutting neoprene]* ZB Laser

Index

Entries in **bold** depict images

First reprinted 2025
The Images Publishing Group Reference Number: IM1772

Published in Australia in 2023 by
The Images Publishing Group Pty Ltd
ABN 89 059 734 431

Offices

Melbourne
Waterman Business Centre
Suite 64, Level 2 UL40
1341 Dandenong Road
Chadstone, Victoria 3148
Australia
Tel: +61 3 8564 8122

New York
6 West 18th Street 4B
New York City, NY 10011
United States
Tel: +1 212 645 1111

Shanghai
6F, Building C,
838 Guangji Road
Hongkou District,
Shanghai 200434
China
Tel: +86 021 31260822

books@imagespublishing.com
www.imagespublishing.com

NATIONAL LIBRARY OF AUSTRALIA

A catalogue record for this book is available from the National Library of Australia

Title: Tectonism: Architecture for the Twenty-First Century // Patrik Schumacher
ISBN: 9781864708967

images Publishing

THE ARTS BRIDGE

This title was commissioned in IMAGES' Melbourne and Shanghai offices to celebrate Patrik Schumacher's achievement as the recipient of the Arts Bridge 2021 Designer of the Year Award.

This book was produced as follows: *Editorial* Georgia (Gina) Tsarouhas, *Art direction* Nicole Boehringer, *Graphic design* Ryan Marshall, *Production* Simon Walsh, Heather Johnson.
Thanks to Maggie Chenhui and Maggie Li (The Arts Bridge).

FSC www.fsc.org MIX Paper | Supporting responsible forestry FSC® C008047

Printed on 140gsm Chinese Golden Sun woodfree FSC® in China by C&C Offset Printing Co., Ltd.